THE DARBY PLAN

FIXING AMERICA'S ECONOMY WITH SMALL BUSINESS

James H. Darby, Jr.

James H. Darby, Jr.
Montgomery AL
www.capitolmusicusa.com
ISBN 978-1-365-67861-5

ACKNOWLEDGEMENTS

I thank all of the employees, past and present, of Capitol Music who strived so hard and stood by me in the past 60+ years. I thank all of the many, many customers whom we have served and whose lives were enriched by music. I thank my family for putting up with a somewhat eccentric workaholic. And I particularly thank my very good friends, journalist Dr. Walt Hines, who helped me edit and publish this book, and technology executive and photographer Elbert Steven Hughes, who so creatively designed the cover.

—JHD

TABLE OF CONTENTS

ABOUT THE AUTHOR

Jim Darby was born and grew up in Florence, Alabama. His forte in school was playing the trumpet, and he earned a music scholarship to college, where he studied engineering and business administration. He played lead trumpet with Holiday on Ice, Ringling Brothers Circus, and several dance bands of the day. He was circulation manager of the *Florence Times* and *Tri-City Daily* newspapers. He was the owner of the Royal Artist Agency, a band booking operation, and began repairing musical instruments in 1947. Today, he is considered one of the best master repairmen of band and orchestra instruments in the country.

In between stints in college, he worked for the US Army Corps of Engineers, returning to college to continue studies in marketing and retailing. His first foray into retailing was with the Ryan Piano Company in Florence, and later he became manager of the Forbes Piano Company. In 1955, he came to Montgomery, Alabama, and opened the Capitol Music Center. The store was very successful in the downtown area and gained popularity throughout the state. In 1988, he moved the store to its present location in east Montgomery, where there was more needed space in a vacated supermarket facility.

Over his many years in business, Jim and Capitol Music have received a myriad of local and state awards for community support and encouragement of musical programs, especially those for school-aged youngsters. There has been national recognition as well. In 2004, *Music Inc.* magazine named Capitol Music among the "Top 50 Music Dealers in the US," out of a total of 8400. Then in 2016, the National Association of Music Manufacturers (NAMM) presented him with its "Believe in Music" award for his "many years of excellent service in the music products industry."

"Darby," as he likes to be called, is an innovator and avid writer, having been published numerous times in various music trade journals and other media. He designed the Darby trumpet, which Blessing still produces today. For years, he has studied swings in the economy and their impact on the music industry. At 87 years of age, he has experienced all of the possible ups and downs of a small businessman, and he is now more concerned than ever about our economy. This is his first effort to put his ideas on how to restore American economic viability in book form.

Walt Hines, MBA, EdD

PREFACE

The backbone of the US economy continues to be small business. So if we are to have a robust economy again, small business must be the principal vehicle. At the same time, we must bring back manufacturing to America, while dealing with the mass merchandisers who have driven many small businesses out of the marketplace, and with the Internet. I understand that in 2016 a greater percentage of Christmas shopping is being done online than ever before.

Additionally, unions have become a huge problem for American business. Labor and trade unions have been a dominant part of the American landscape since the late 1800s. As a small business owner in Alabama, I never had to contend directly with union membership among my employees, but the unions clearly have had something to do with the prices I had to pay to stock instruments and related products in my store. This really was not a big problem until the last couple of decades when rapidly rising personnel, production, and transportation costs began to translate into significant increases in wholesale prices. While the big box stores could get quantity discounts, the small retailers had to meet the higher prices in order to maintain their dealerships.

Most dealers like me rely on bank loans to buy merchandise in the quantities required and then pay off the loans as the merchandise sells. But with the ongoing recession, banks are not making these loans anymore. Countless small music stores have failed. I, myself, am managing to barely hang on, largely due to a large inventory of used instruments that can be reconditioned and sold.

Labor unions have increasingly brought about higher and higher costs of products and services, and public sector unions have given us higher and higher costs of government. This means that governments at all levels require more and more money from the private sector to run their programs. Obviously, this translates into higher taxes.

Then there's the matter of governmental regulations, again at all levels. Even in colonial times, when provincial legislatures enacted caps on wages and commodity prices, there were impacts on business. Municipal licenses were required for master craftsmen. But for the most part, these early regulations served to promote business. Beginning with the Sherman Antitrust Act of 1890, however, there came a succession of regulations that have many times hampered businesses, both large and small. We now have thousands and thousands of rules and regulations that impinge on all businesses. Unfortunately, it's the small businesses that can least afford to comply.

In 1955, going into business was relatively simple. It was similar to getting married. In fact, my wife and I together formed the Capitol Music Center in downtown Montgomery, Alabama, and have continued to keep it going for over 60 years. What makes a business successful is the same type of thing that makes a marriage successful. In other words, the same qualities apply to both endeavors—openness, transparency, honesty, showing love, caring, being outgoing, and giving of self to others. Granted, these qualities are not always present in either business or marriage, but some might succeed anyway. I am simply sharing what I have learned. The bottom line is that it takes teamwork—husband and wife, dealer and customer, supplier and dealer. Each must understand and respect the other. Marriage should not be an adversarial relationship. Neither should business.

We need to save the American family, and we want to save America. If the government can take care of national security, the path for economic recovery is small business. The motivation is love—love of country, love of freedom, love of family, love of business, love of fellow man. Our future depends on the decisions we make right now. This book is about giving solid hope to our children and grandchildren for a prosperous future. The purpose of this book is to educate the reader by revealing what is going on in today's business world and the impact it is having and by sharing what I believe is needed to restore economic viability.

This book is dedicated to you—your children, your family, your life, your country, your future, your dreams, your finances, your happiness, your business. We all know that the American family has been under attack from many fronts for years. Part and parcel of saving the American family is saving the family (small) business. Some of the thoughts presented herein might seem like wild ideas at first because they are certainly radical departures from what we have been doing in our country. I would hope that readers will have an open mind and follow these thoughts out to the end.

Above all, this book is a work of love, perhaps the final installment in a long life devoted to serving others. It is a work committed to salvaging the American economy and our way of life before it becomes too late to do so. It is about giving real hope to our children and grandchildren and their future.

A large part of the contents of this book derives from my own experiences. After all, I lived through the Great Depression, several wars, and thirteen presidents, so I know what happened. At the same time, I want to provide some historical perspective of educational value. Hence, I am including a chapter on the history of small business and one on the problems posed by unions, governmental regulations, quantity discount merchandisers, and the Internet.

On November 8, 2016, eminent businessman Donald Trump was decisively elected by the American people to be the 45th President of the United States. He has pledged to bring back the economy "big time." This development may well prove to be the real stimulus we have needed for significant and enduring corrections finally to take place.

Jim Darby

Chapter 1

ABOUT THE BOOK

PURPOSE

The backbone of the US economy continues to be small business. Indeed, small businesses represent over 95% of all firms and provide jobs for more than half of the private sector work force. Over the last decade, small businesses have generated 60-80% of new jobs annually.[1] The present state of our economy dictates that small businesses somehow must be stimulated and energized for a recovery to take place. Bailouts and government takeovers of big corporations are not the answer.

I have discovered that most people, including most politicians, who are not in business have no idea of how the business world operates. So, I am going to expose what goes on in the confidential business world and share my foolproof formula for creating jobs and building a solid business base for our country.

Rebuilding opportunities for small business is the key ingredient, assuming that getting our country out of debt is a national goal and that government spending at current levels is quickly brought under control. Another ingredient is bringing manufacturing back to America. Still another is dealing with the mass merchandisers who have already driven many small businesses out of the marketplace, and with the Internet, where more and more of America's business is being conducted. From the perspective of a Top 50 small businessman, I am going to share the secrets that are destroying the country's economy in almost a racketeering manner. Millions have been hurt by the excess profits of the quantity discount (QD) mass merchandisers, and they don't even know it. And now, unprecedented government spending is changing the economic landscape, perhaps irretrievably. American manufacturers, small businesses, and the public are in great peril.

So, my purpose is to unleash the full power and potential of small business in America. If somehow the government could concentrate only on its Constitutional duties and responsibilities, like national security, then it might be possible to clear a path for economic recovery led by small business. The motivation is love—love of country, love of freedom, love of family, love of business, love of fellow man. Our future depends on the decisions we make right now. This book is about giving solid hope to our children and grandchildren for a prosperous future.

INTRODUCTION

In a capitalist system, all business needs to be profitable. That means that you must be able to pay for the goods you sell, the wages of the employees you hire or outside services you use, all your other expenses, and then have enough profit to make it worthwhile for you to have your money invested in the business. All that means a lot of hard work, good judgment, frugality, and tenacity. For all your work and the risks you take, you should be able to make a reasonable profit, and you should be able to do that in an honest and noble way. And mark well my words— my wife and I built our business ourselves, regardless of claims otherwise by President Obama.

This book is about creating jobs, building a solid business base for our country, and getting our country out of debt. We must bring manufacturing back to America and renew opportunities for small businesses. The playing field has to be leveled so that small business can compete with the quantity discount (QD) merchandisers. Consideration must be given to placing duties or some type of limitation on foreign imports. The sales tax structure has to be revised so as not to penalize local retailers while Internet or out-of-state suppliers do not have to pay a sales tax.

At first I was not going to use any personal experiences in writing this book. However, I changed my mind and decided to use examples from my personal life to emphasize key points. I have lived it for all of 87 years, so why not share it?

I guess that the start of my business career was at the age of eight, when my father sat me down and said, "Son, this is your eighth birthday, which means that you are getting to be a man. Getting to be a man means that after two weeks you will have to be on your own spending money. No longer will you be getting your spending money from your mother and me." As I sat up a bit more erectly, my dad "set me up."

Bob Plowden, who lived on Olive Street, had a *Birmingham Age Herald* paper route (early in the morning before seven) that he was about to give up and turn over to his as yet unnamed helper. Coach Brawley, who lived on Sherrod Avenue, had been looking for someone to cut his grass. Right down the street from him was the big apartment building that my buddy Jimmy Young's crippled father had, and he had been looking for someone to stoke the furnace, wash woodwork and windows, and keep the building up. I took all three jobs, and I have been a workaholic ever since. This was the nicest thing that my dad ever did for me. In addition to earning my spending money,

I found that helping others provides true meaning for one's life.

Our elected officials, regardless of party, do not seem to be able to focus on the pressing substantive issues facing the country and the American people, i.e., national security, debt reduction, economic strength, and assurance of individual freedoms guaranteed by the Constitution. Instead, attention is being devoted almost exclusively to the complete overhaul of our health care system, which was already the best system in the world and which more than 90% of Americans were happy with. This effort will not save our economy but will further damage it, perhaps permanently. How do we wake up the members of Congress to tend to their rightful obligations to the America people and to shepherd the legislation needed to address America's real problems?

Saving small business (restoring our economic strength and leadership) is what this book is about. The salvation of our country hangs in the balance, and Americans in all walks of life must deal with it now or face losing the momentum of the greatest and most successful societal experiment in the history of the world. This book is an exposé by a "Top 50 in America" businessman of the confidential secrets that are destroying the country in a racketeering manner. Excess profits and corruption in many big companies and the advent of the quantity discounters and Internet retailing have had an adverse impact on our manufacturing base, our small businesses, and the general public. The American people need to know what is going on in the business world. I will define who has been hurt and what can be done about it, with specific concentration on the small business arena.

BRICK AND MORTAR

I am of the school that, if you do things for others (give of yourself to others), enough will come back home to take care of you. It's kind of corny, I know, but it's called "showing love." (I'm not alone in this claim—a current TV automobile commercial notes that "Love: It's what makes a Subaru a Subaru.") We will pay for our advertisements in the concert programs, the football programs, or the school annuals, knowing that these programs will never generate a single sale, but we do this as a public service to support the schools.

Before any instrument is given to the customer, it goes through our shop, and I personally check everyone's work. Just because something is brand new does not necessarily mean that it works properly or is as good as it was designed to be. That's the world that we live in today, so we pick up where the manufacturers leave off. When that instrument leaves my store, I want it to sing, to be the best it can be. This little bit extra might make the difference in whether or not the student finds the instrument enjoyable to practice or the professional musician feels confident to pass a demanding audition.

When the band directors have their meetings, they know they can count on Capitol Music to pick up the bill. If an instrument gets torn up, and it happens just before a concert or all-state competition, the director knows that, if necessary, Jim Darby will work all night to do the repairs for a token fee so that the "show can go on." If it is an emergency, we might drive a hundred miles just to deliver a few reeds before the performance. When the band goes to all-state competition, they know that Capitol Music will be there with repairs or loaner instruments if something gets damaged or quits playing. Most of the time, all of this is done without charging anything.

It is highly unlikely that one would get this kind of service from a mass merchandiser. Most of the time this type of thing goes on without any fanfare or publicity—it's all just part of giving good service. When you are sick, you would like to find the best doctor you can. You are not likely to find this type of qualified specialist in a mass merchandising store. In fact, you can only rarely find highly trained and competent personnel who really care about the customer in a mass merchandise store. Thus, the service component goes by the wayside.

I am an entrepreneur. I care about my store, and I love and care about my customers. Like my own store, smaller businesses on the whole have a qualified, trained staff that is able to deliver a level of one-on-one service and assistance that mass merchandisers cannot. I am brick and mortar; I help build the community. This is part of what my store does for the public. I provide large inventories of new and used instruments, student to professional quality, less expensive to more expensive. Customers can try out an instrument on the spot or check it out on approval if they are in doubt. They may purchase or rent the instrument, with a rent-to-own option at no finance charge, and they all get free minor repairs for 24 months.

For many years in the past, I have normally gone out to the schools two days a week to repair band instruments as a public service, free of charge. We still go out to visit the band directors once a week, take care of emergency repairs, and help the directors in any way they might need. We will loan them specialized instruments—bells, chimes, tympani, and other percussion—for special concerts or occasions. We will make presentations to the student body about playing musical instruments and will test the students, free of charge, to determine which instrument might be best for them. And if a student has a burning desire to play an instrument, and even if his or her parents' credit record is questionable, more often than not Capitol Music can provide that instrument.

Good service is what good retailing is all about. The mass merchandisers aren't going to provide this level of service, but it is the heart and soul of a small business. It is what people remember, and it creates fierce loyalty to and support of service-oriented establishments. Moreover, there accrues a great feeling of satisfaction from honing your skills and striving to develop yourself so that you may become the best there is in your line of work. When you get there, your reputation spreads. You can't buy this type of advertising; you earn it. This is the true American spirit. May it live forever in the greatest country the world has ever known!

GENESIS OF THE BOOK

The initial draft of this book was typed on a really old Royal typewriter. At age 87, I am more comfortable with the old machine that I learned to type on. It was the ribbon on this typewriter that led to the book. You see, when the old ribbon finally gave up the ghost, I went to one of the quantity discount mass-merchandising office supply houses for a replacement ribbon. I had called ahead, and they said they had the ribbon in stock. However, when I got to the store, they had a smaller size Royal ribbon rather than the size I needed. Inquiring of them where I might find the correct ribbon, I was informed that the Internet would probably be the only place to find one. Looking in the classified section of the phone book, I found a typewriter repair business, and I called them. They said they could take care of my need.

The business was located in a section of town that was previously residential but had been rezoned for business. The establishment was packed full of all types of new and used office machines with a single aisle leading back to the office and the repair department. Although quite crowded, the store was clean and neatly organized. I even spotted an old, gray, used Royal typewriter exactly like the one I have. I was warmly greeted by a middle-aged, somewhat portly black gentleman who obviously was the proprietor. When he went back to locate the part, he did not find the exact size that I needed. It appeared to me that he had precisely the same size that I had earlier seen in the super store. At this point, he could have said the same thing as the super store clerk, but not this gentleman. In the true spirit of entrepreneurial excellence, he assured me that he could still take care of my requirement.

He then took my larger size spool and removed the old ribbon, informing me that the ribbon on the smaller spool that he had was the same size and length as was on my larger spool. In a very skilled and patient manner, he rolled the ribbon from his spool onto my spool. When I asked him if he wanted me to hold one of the spools, he declined, explaining that he appreciated my offer but that he did not want me to get ink on my hands. When he had finished, the charge was only $4.50. Now whom do you think I will call first the next time I need anything this retail "giant" might have? He exemplified going that extra mile in service with a positive attitude and giving of his expertise in a loving and caring way. We must put a framework in place to perpetuate this type of entrepreneurship. This is the kind of service that built our country—the true American way.

Just as we need to recapture the service attitude in the marketplace, we need to return to quality manufacturing in our country. "Made in America" does not carry the same clout that it once did. At one time, it meant that you could not buy anything better. An American product was well worth the price even if you might have to pay more for it. It was made to exacting standards by people who took great pride in their company, their workmanship, and the superior design and lasting quality built into the product. In their quest for cheap products, the quantity discount mass merchants are causing the demise of the traditional quality, work ethic, and skill levels once connoted by "made in America."

HOW THE BOOK IS STRUCTURED

Following this introductory chapter, there is a chapter briefly describing the history of small business in America, one on the business environment when I started my store in 1955, and what happened thereafter. Next, is a chapter on the present situation in which we find ourselves and the problems that make it so difficult, often ruinous, for small business today. I devote a separate chapter to one of those problems, i.e., how the quantity discount (QD) system evolved, followed by a chapter on the secret price lists that have been in play from the start of my own business and other confidential practices inspired by the QD mass merchant movement. Finally, I present a chapter outlining solutions to the problems identified and a plan for implementing them.

Chapter 2

A BRIEF HISTORY OF SMALL BUSINESS IN THE USA

The American story essentially began with two tiny settlements: Jamestown, Virginia, and Plymouth, Massachusetts. As more and more colonists arrived, other settlements came into being, and between 1607 and 1733 these settlements evolved into 13 colonies along the eastern coast of the new land which were owned and controlled by European kings, principally English kings. The kings had financed the over-the-ocean journey of their people who wanted a new life, and they expected a return on their investment. Trading companies were established to profit from such New World goods as tobacco and other crops in the South and furs and timbers in the North. In fact, it was tobacco that saved the struggling settlement of Jamestown, and by 1627 the growers there were sending 250 tons annually of the rich leaves to England. The region was so fertile for tobacco cultivation that the plants even grew along the streets.[1]

Many of the initial settlers were farmers, but there were also ministers, various laborers, and businessmen, people both rich and poor. Each settlement was populated by a fairly compatible group of people, and there existed a cooperative spirit among them. Everyone gathered together to build houses, churches, schools, and other town buildings. Every community had many needs, and it soon became difficult for each and every family to be completely self-sufficient. It was not long until blacksmiths, cobblers, carpenters, and all sorts of tradesmen set up shops. Coopers made barrels for shipping tobacco overseas.

Weaving houses were set up where women transformed flax and hemp into material for clothes.[2]

Shipping ports dotted the map all along the eastern seacoast, and a class of merchants emerged to do business at these ports. Goods sent to Europe were traded for clothes, furniture, coaches, books, toys, farming tools, building materials, etc., from the "old country." By the year 1690, there were five colonial towns, all of them seaports, which had grown to the point that they soon would be considered "big" cities—Boston, Newport, Charleston, Philadelphia, and New York (originally named New Amsterdam by the Dutch settlers). New York had a population of 3,900 and Philadelphia 4,000. By the turn of the century, new arrivals into the colonies included masons, carpenters, tailors, butchers, millers, tanners, locksmiths, saddlers, glass blowers, hatters, engravers, brickmakers, silversmiths, potters, and weavers of cloth, linen, and stockings. These tradesmen set up small shops in the cities, worked on plantations, or traveled from village to village selling their wares.[3]

So, the very first businesses in the new country were small, mom-and-pop type stores, specialty shops, farms, and itinerant tradesmen. All of the trades listed above were included, and there were livery stables, carriage makers, general stores, boarding houses, hotels, stagecoach offices, newspaper presses, and even restaurants among the early businesses. And of course, any town of any size at all had a bank and a tavern or saloon. On the farms and in rural areas, men and women operated "home industries," in which they made candles, soap, and woven cloths that they took to town and sold on market days. Every business that existed at that time in fact was a small business, and virtually all employment was in small businesses.[4]

Small business continued to be the basis of the American economy until the Industrial Revolution took hold, at which point big business became a factor. This revolution, made possible by the steam engine and textile machinery, actually started in England around 1770. A number of important inventions came into play, but one of the more propitious of these came from a family of ironmasters, the Darbys. This English family figured out how to transform coal into coke as a more efficient fuel for smelting. Soon the factory system was established, and by the 1850s Englishmen for the most part were working in industrialized towns, bringing far-reaching changes to their lives. This revolution then advanced in Belgium and France, and later in the United States. Slow to proceed at first, by the early 1900s the United States was leading all other nations in industrialization.[5]

In the meantime, President Thomas Jefferson in 1804 had sent Lewis and Clark on an expedition which ended up on the Pacific coast and established the western boundary of the United States.[6] Western expansion began shortly thereafter, as pioneers ventured into the vast expanse to establish homesteads and to farm the fertile land. Small farming enterprises came into being, and with the development of towns and cities in the western frontier, merchants, craftsmen, and professionals also set up small businesses.[7] During the same general period, three industries emerged—the railroad, steamboat[8], and telegraph[9] industries. These were the beginnings of big business in America, and they continued to expand throughout the 1800s. With the impetus of the Industrial Revolution in the 1900s, big business was here to stay.

During the American Civil War (1861-1865), advanced machinery was used for the first time to produce large quantities of uniforms, shoes, and rifles for the soldiers. But it was not until World War I (1914-1918) that the Industrial Revolution sprang to life in the United States.[10] Here began a period of mass production, technology, large-scale manufacturing, and scientific management, the most notable proponent of which was Frederick Taylor, as any student of management should know.[11] Once underway, the progress of the revolution advanced in the United States at a faster pace than in any other country,[12] the result of which was that we became the greatest industrial force in the world and, in turn, we attained the highest standard of living among all nations.

An interesting sideline was the landmark Rock Island Bridge Case in 1856-1857. Up until that time, steamboats operated unimpeded on virtually every river in the country. However, the railroad lines were rapidly moving west, and they were building their own bridges over rivers. After the Rock Island Bridge was built across the Mississippi River in the early 1850s, a steamboat owner sued, claiming that the bridge limited river navigation. (The steamboat Effie Afton had actually collided with one of the bridge's piers.)[13] Representing the railroad company was a 47-year-old lawyer named Abraham Lincoln, who won the case.[14] An ultimate result, among other things, was that hinges had to be installed on steamboat smokestacks so that they could be lowered in order to pass under the bridges.

In the 1920s, big companies like AT&T, Standard Oil of New Jersey, GE, and DuPont made huge accomplishments of scale, but small business was still the mainstay of the American economy.[15] Tradesmen all across the expanding nation continued to grow and thrive, small shops of all kinds were successful, and the traveling salesman had established his place in history. Of particular interest to this author were the salesmen who went from town to town selling band instruments. The Broadway play *Music Man* was all about such a salesman, circa 1912, who wound up in fictitious River City, Iowa, and there was probably more fact than fiction in the sales approach depicted in this delightful story.[16] America was riding high in the "Roaring 20s."

Then came the Great Depression, beginning with the stock market crash of 1929. All of a sudden, within a four-year period, some 13 million working and middle class Americans lost their jobs. It was a devastating period that adversely affected all businesses, both great and small—some 26,000 businesses collapsed in the first year.[17] Corrective measures taken by Presidents Hoover and Roosevelt did not help much to turn the economy about, and many observers now say that their increased taxation and big government spending "initiatives" may have actually prolonged the depression.[18] At any rate, it was not until the advent of WWII, in conjunction with the positive impact of continuing industrialization, that conditions really changed and an economic turnaround occurred. By 1942, the American economic engine was once again charging full steam ahead to support the war effort and to restore business and industrial capacity.[19]

By 1957, there were thousands of giant corporations in operation. But of the four million business enterprises in the United States at that time, most of them were small establishments owned and run by one, two, or perhaps several people in partnership.[20] Accordingly, a significant level of employment continued to be in small businesses, and on an annual basis over the years, small business has consistently accounted for most of the new jobs created nationwide. In 1958, the small business share of the GDP was right at 57 percent.[21] Small business remained strong and durable up to and throughout the early 1970s.

After one year of the Jimmy Carter presidency (1976-1980), the economy took a severe downturn. By 1980, inflation at 18% had driven the cost of living up by 48%. Home mortgage rates were as high as 20-21%. There was a shortage of gasoline, and Carter's national speed limit of 55mph failed to help. The negative impact on small business was significant. Emblematic of Carter's initiatives that hurt this economic sector was his Small Business Energy Loan Act of 1978, the purpose of which was to involve small firms in solar energy and energy conservation. There were little or no takers. It was during this time that big discount houses began to emerge, and many small businesses couldn't compete. Carter signed into law the Small Business Investment Incentive Act of 1980, but by then it was too late.

Ronald Reagan cut taxes and reduced impediments on small business at the beginning of his presidency in 1981. With new confidence, small business thrived in the 1980s due to its ability to innovate and customize products, provide on-the-spot customer service, and adapt to changes in the economy without having to contend with managerial bureaucracy and unions.[22] In 1995, there was a total of 22.5 million independent business enterprises in the United States, only 4.5 million of which were corporations. The rest were non-farm sole proprietorships (16.4 million) and partnerships (1.6 million).[23]

With the enactment of "free trade" policies by the Bush 41 administration, "the U.S, has lost millions of jobs to out-sourcing, as U.S.-based multinational corporations have pursued cheap foreign labor....The basic formula is that the United States has exported high-paying manufacturing jobs to foreign nations, while a Spanish-speaking underclass from south of the border has been imported to compete at lower benefits and wages for low-skilled jobs in the United States. The loser in this equation is the U.S. middle class...."[24] And who owns and operates the bulk of our small businesses? You guessed it—the US middle class.

From that time through 2007, the American economy in general continued to grow, albeit in a different direction. Small business endured despite the new competition from mass merchandisers, who were able to obtain quantity discounts unavailable to small retailers, from manufacturers, and from the Internet, where local retailers' prices can be undercut routinely. In 2006, some 77 percent of US employment was attributed to small business.[25] Historically, 60-80 percent of all new jobs are created by small business.[26] In 2010, in the midst of the Obama recession, those numbers dropped considerably.[27]

Clearly, small business remains a substantial part of the economy and an important key to recovery; yet, all efforts thus far have been directed to huge bailouts and stimulus programs for banks and big corporations in addition to unprecedented expansion of government size and spending. As was found with similar measures enacted by both Hoover and Roosevelt, heavy taxation and big government spending are not going to work this time either.[28] If our governments at all levels really want to help the poor and promote economic recovery, they would concentrate on making things easier for small businesses by reducing taxes and burdensome regulations, or what one author calls "a small-business renaissance."[29]

Chapter 3

HOW IT WAS AND WHAT HAPPENED

HOW IT WAS

I went into business for myself in 1955 by establishing a retail music dealership in Montgomery, Alabama. At that time, the "in thing" was to play a musical instrument. Public school enrollment was overflowing, and the music budgets were being expanded and adequately funded. As a result, schools had very large bands and orchestras, stage bands, and myriads of small musical groups. Famous name dance bands of the swing era—Benny Goodman, the Dorseys, Les Brown, Ray Anthony, Duke Ellington, Tex Beneke, Stan Kenton, Harry James, Ralph Flanagan, Russ Morgan, etc.—were still touring. Elvis Presley and the Beatles were just coming onto the scene. Everywhere, people were playing guitars, pianos, organs, and recorders, as well as the entire array of band and orchestral instruments. Even football and basketball players were in their school bands and orchestras. There were many community chamber groups, and live music was available in every club. Live concerts were drawing thousands throughout the country, and record and sheet music sales were booming.

Interest rates were favorable, and loans for the purchase of musical instruments were easily financed through lending institutions. The music industry was expanding, and manufacturers were running at full capacity with new businesses springing up everywhere. The expansion of retailers, jobbers, and manufacturers alike meant that master orders had to be placed early in the year in the hope of having adequate stock for the peak selling seasons. Stringed instruments, pianos, and organs were so popular that they began to become "impulse items," spawning the growth of music retailers in high traffic malls and shopping centers. We were riding the "baby boom" for all it was worth, and many in the industry apparently thought it would last forever.

For the most part, governmental regulations at the time facilitated a favorable business climate, and retail prices could be set and protected. A good franchise literally assured success for a retailer in his protected territory. Over the ensuing 35 years, my full-service music business, Capitol Music, flourished and became one of the largest and best-known retail outlets in the southeast. It was an enduring source of consistent employment for some 10-12 full-time sales and service personnel. Then the whole environment began to change, and not for the better.

WHAT HAPPENED

By the 1990s, the large school bands of the "good old days" had become smaller. Salary increases for teachers had placed additional strain on schools' already inflated financial budgets, and we found that when money becomes tight, the first places considered for budget cuts are music and art. So, thousands of people had musical instruments left over from the big band days stored in closets and attics. When these instruments were sold in yard sales or through classified ads and shoppers' bulletins, they were generally not priced at their true worth. The philosophy was to price them at "what they would move at," which in most cases was a token amount of the fair price that a music merchant would ask for the item. For example, a band director who was a regular customer showed me a Bach Stradivarius silver-plated trumpet, which he had purchased for $35 in a yard sale. This trumpet at the time listed for somewhat over $3000. What had evolved was that, in many band recruiting programs, the largest percentage of the instruments were not being sold by the dealer but were being purchased in the community from former band members for about the same amount a dealer would charge for a three-to-six-month rental.

For a number of reasons, Americans weren't having as many children as before. Moreover, those families with the most children were living in the less affluent, even impoverished segments of our society. Population shifts were occurring away from the urban areas to the suburbs of our cities, and private schools were springing up everywhere. Comparatively few of these private schools could financially support a good school music program, and this additional loss of already decreased public school enrollment further cut public funding for music programs. Geographically, businesses that concentrated their efforts in the downtown area found that they had to significantly adjust their focus.

What could be more efficient than the central shopping districts of yore surrounded by the residential areas? But by the 1990s, most inner-city or downtown shopping areas were forsaken, dead, or dying. Our cities became the epitome of inefficiency as we traveled north, east, south, or west from one extreme side of the city to another in our daily life patterns. Untold hours of travel time and, therefore, increased transportation expenses became the rule in practically all of our lives. Thus, less money was available in family budgets for such things as musical instruments and other discretionary items.

As money got tight and interest rates grew, many lending institutions ceased to finance musical instruments for dealers, and floor plans (stocking large instruments on delayed payment arrangements) became economically infeasible for all concerned. Government regulations changed with respect to territorial and price protection, and we awakened to a whole new era.

ENTER THE MASS MERCHANDISING DISCOUNTERS

Not that the retailers did not have enough woes already, but the new rules and regulations relaxing territorial and price protection rang the death knell for many dealers, and the way was then clear for the mass merchandisers to evolve onto the scene. Slowly at first, and then progressively faster, the public and the mass merchandisers began to find each other. (This connection would be aided in a major way by the advent of the Internet, but more about that in a later chapter.)

The mass-merchandising discounters' advertisements penetrated the market through direct mailings to the band directors and school officials. Their ads were also in the music magazines and all kinds of other publications, as well as in classified telephone directories listing WATS lines. They achieved virtually 100% penetration of the market. Just about every student had or had access to the discounters' catalogs, and many band directors made the catalogs readily available, often displaying them on their bulletin boards with the admonition to note the prices and try to get a better price from the local dealer. Respected music merchants, who had spent years in building their reputations for service, integrity, and reliability, suddenly had their positive images questioned and in some cases destroyed. They became the "rip-off dealer" in the eyes of many customers.

In addition to the impact on the local dealer's image and on the competitive structure, most out-of-state mass merchandisers had the advantage of not having to charge sales tax, which afforded a 3-10% discount (now 10% or more in most places) right off the top on a given sale. As long as the out-of-state discounter did not have a representative in the state wherein a purchaser resided, he did not have to collect sales tax. This was patently unfair to the local dealers. Technically, it is the responsibility of the purchaser to voluntarily pay the sales tax due to his local tax office, but that rarely happens. Thus, the tax revenues on these sales did not (and still do not) make their way back into the budgets of local schools and other tax funded programs. The government, in essence, was rewarding the out-of-state discounters for not having a representative to service the purchaser and penalizing the local merchant for employing service-oriented representatives. Again, not a fair arrangement!

Due to the foregoing and other factors, some music retailers have gone out of business just like the corner grocery stores that we all loved. Still others are being threatened even more severely than ever before by the current recession. Yet, if manufacturers and distributors in the music industry continue to exercise sound judgment, responsibility, and integrity, there is hope that they can implement necessary changes to deal with the evolving challenges to their enterprises and to local retailers and thus save a vital sector of our economy. What are those changes? A later chapter will be devoted to this subject.

ROOT HAIRS

Some time ago I had to remove a very large oak tree (roots and all) from a building site. Seven or eight large roots were spreading out from the tree trunk, obviously feeding and supporting the mighty oak. As we dug around the tree, it was amazing to see the thousands of tiny root hairs, each doing its job of reaching out and finding sustenance for the tree. Most people would look at the great oak and tend to overlook the tiny root hairs that were the real support system. How akin is the mighty oak to the music industry!

I could not help comparing the large oak tree to the music industry manufacturers who would possibly consider seven or eight huge mass merchandising discounters (the large roots) to be sufficient underpinning for their operations. What the manufacturers are missing is the fact that each of those large roots is dependent on the fruits of the labor of thousands of root hairs (the retailers). Destroy these root hairs and soon the whole tree dies.

Hometown and neighborhood music merchants are the root hairs of the industry, and they are daily promoting, advertising, and reaching out, i.e., providing every possible source of sustenance (business) for the music industry. These root hair merchants are where it really happens—in the schools and the teaching studios, in contacts with private teachers, amateurs and working musicians, constantly encouraging and supporting them. The root hair retailers service and repair instruments and work with school boards, principals, superintendents, band parents, booster groups, churches, and purchasing committees. Clearly, they are an important conduit in the community.

Root hair dealers invest in inventory and maintain a showroom so that potential purchasers can see, touch, try and feel the merchandise with helpful assistance from a salesperson. On-scene sales personnel help the customer decide on the right merchandise and assist with the details of the purchase. The local dealer is there to repair and service the equipment as needed and otherwise provide support following the purchase. (Discounters and Internet sellers cannot do this.) Learning to play a musical instrument is not an overnight proposition, and most of the time progress is so slow that the player needs the encouragement and moral support of both the local dealer and the teacher.

The mass-merchandising discounter is not creating a sustained business relationship, as price is the main thing he has to sell. He is leeching sales away from the local retailer, who for generations has helped to plant the seed of desire for playing music in the mind of the customer in the first place. Manufacturers and jobbers must have enough wisdom, knowledge and understanding to be able to have a broad view of how a sale is created. Then, they need to support the root hair system that "makes it happen." Consideration given to supporting the local retailer is going to reap long-term dividends to the entire industry.

The music industry needs more people purchasing musical instruments. Consider the thousands of youngsters and adults who will not have the desire or opportunity to play an instrument if the root hair dealers are driven to extinction. As our society advances technologically, we will see more and more of the dehumanization of people, and this is where our market will be in the future. The therapeutic value of creating music will become more of a vital necessity to mankind's mental health. The local music merchant, not the mass merchandiser, is the "one-on-one" type of counselor needed to help the customer find the optimum musical outlet. It's as individual as seeing your doctor or having your suit properly tailored—things a distant discount house or Internet site is unable to do.

If the current trends continue to the point where a handful of national discounters have the dominant part of the market, manufacturers may wake up to a different world than they ever imagined. Of course, I realize there are a number of success books out there espousing the admonition to drop small accounts and go after the big bucks. They contend that small accounts usually stay small and that time and effort are better spent on the big accounts. It would be naïve to think the mass merchandising discounters are going away; they are here to stay. However, there is still tremendous strength in a network of many root hair retailers. The root hair merchants traditionally have been the backbone of the American economy, and the root hair music retailers have been the backbone of the music industry.

For a manufacturer, there is great strength in a large network of root hair retailers who cannot dictate to the manufacturer either prices or policy. By contrast, if the industry evolves to the place where a few national discounters control the market, those discounters then will be in a position to also control the manufacturer. They will be able to dictate product price and profit structure such that the manufacturer will either have to comply with their demands or go out of business.

MULTILEVEL QUANTITY DISCOUNTS: A BIG PROBLEM

Recently, I witnessed a scenario that probably happens in the music industry more often than we would like to think. I was in the Birmingham, Ala., office of one of America's largest electronics and appliance manufacturers where I was purchasing electrical supplies, when a gentleman came in seeking to buy over $100,000 worth of small motors. He had prices from three other manufacturers and was prepared to pay cash. This was the first time they had ever seen or heard of this person; yet they sold him the motors at a heavily discounted price. After the transaction was completed, the manager, who was a personal friend of mine, confided that he had sold the motors at a price just slightly above the actual cost of manufacture. He did not want his competitors to get the order, and he considered this to be a one-time deal. He said, "I can't afford to sell to my regular dealers at this price, and I know he is going to cut their throats; however, we are no longer all that concerned about the future—we are concerned about right now!" Of course, the legality of this sort of thing is highly suspect. Just how many times does this kind of "under-the-counter" deal go on within our industry? I have attended several bid openings where the school's bid price was ridiculously below any published maximum quantity discount schedule available to dealers.

Some time ago we received a huge shipment of Christmas musical merchandise that we had not ordered, from a large Chicago jobber. After some phone calls, we found out that the jobber had made an invoicing error and had sent the order to Capitol Music (my store) rather than Capitol Wholesale (a local discount department store). We also received the invoice for the shipment, and it was a real shocker! The cost price was by far less than any that we had ever seen on the same merchandise from that jobber. When I talked to the president of the jobbing house, he told me that he was very sorry but that I could not buy at that price. This pricing was not available to the music industry; it was only available to discount department stores. In protest, we discontinued doing business with that jobber. That's all we could do about it.

One of the inequities of the multi-level quantity discount system is that no consideration is given to the size of the retailer's trading area, the saturation of that market area, and the economic inequities of different areas. The "Po-Dunk" retailer in a sparsely populated, drought, or poverty stricken community cannot be competitive in price because he is required to purchase the same quantity of merchandise to get a maximum discount as the metropolitan retailer with a larger population and a trading area of high employment and general economic affluence. In addition, the big metropolitan retailer is probably pulling in mail order and/or Internet business from well outside his trading area, indeed, from all across the country.

Without the quantity discount (QD) system, consideration could be given by the manufacturer to the conditions in a trading area when setting up a dealership. (This assumes, of course, that the Federal Government is not going to take over the manufacturing company and thus control where dealerships will be located and who will have them.) The purchase of a certain minimum number of units could be required to become a franchised dealer, which would tend to keep the product(s) stocked in legitimate music stores. Beyond this minimum quantity parameter, all dealers could be placed on the same equal cost schedule without any quantity discounts. In this way, every retailer would have a level playing field for the conduct of his business.

The multilevel quantity discount policy of manufacturers and distributors, by its very nature, spawns the transshipping of products between dealers. The music marketplace demands a great variety of products, and what retailer can afford to stock enough of every manufacturer's products to get the maximum discount level needed to be competitive in that arena? The natural outgrowth of the multilevel quantity discount policy is that one retailer will contact another retailer in a different geographical location and say, "I am on maximum discount with company A and you are on maximum discount with company B, so let's be smart and work with each other. I will ship A's products to you at my cost if you will ship to me B's products at your cost. This benefits us both in terms of having additional products to sell and allowing us both to reach the maximum volumes levels with the respective manufacturers."

To counter the QD system, many successful retailers have joined or created "buying groups." This is where a number of retailers are located far enough away from each other so that they do not consider themselves competitors. These retailers form a buying group in order to combine their individual stock orders all together to reach quantity discount levels that they would be unable to achieve as individual stores. My good friend, Raymond Cohen, president of Cohen's Electronics and Appliances, participates beneficially in one of these buying groups. Of course, this necessitates some additional expense of administration and other requirements of the group. Under our present system, this is the only way many stores are able to compete with the larger QD mass merchants.

QD, however, is not the only problem small businesses face. The next chapter addresses these problems in considerable detail.

Chapter 4

HOW IT IS: THE PROBLEMS

Problems facing today's small businessman are fourfold: government regulations, unions, multilevel quantity discounts, and the Internet.

GOVERNMENT REGULATIONS

Since 2002, there have been more than 70,000 various federal regulations enacted each year that affect American businesses in one way or another. In two years of the Obama Administration, those regulations have exceeded 80,000. These regulations are documented in the Federal Register.[1] In 2008, the Small Business Administration (SBA) estimated that the cost of such regulations was $1.75T.[2] That's a huge price tag for our businesses to have to bear.

So what's the impact of these regulations? A plethora of agencies, such as the EPA, OSHA, DOE, NHTSA, NLRB, FDA, IRS, etc., as well as many laws that Congress has passed, like Obamacare (ACA) and Dodd-Frank, all place certain burdens on American businesses. For example, in 2011 armed federal agents of the Justice Department raided Gibson Guitar plants in Nashville and Memphis because the Environmental Investigation Agency (EIA) claimed they were importing illegal rosewood from Madagascar in violation of the Lacey Act. The factories were evacuated, production was shut down, the employees were sent home, and wood was confiscated.[3] Similar raids were conducted in 2009 when federal agents seized Gibson's stock of ebony wood. Turns out that all of the wood used in Gibson guitars is properly certified and legal. (Isn't it interesting how the DOJ can track and find imported wood in guitar plants but can't seem to figure out where millions of illegal immigrants are or how they got here?)

The FDA, for another example, projects that food service companies will have to devote something like 14 million hours annually to comply with requirements that vending machines and restaurant menus contain the calorie count on each item sold.[4] I remember hearing about federal agents raiding an Amish farm at 5 a.m. one morning in 2010 for selling unauthorized raw milk. In July, 2015, it was reported on Fox News that a barbeque restaurant in Austin TX may have to close because its smoke was not being confined to its immediate property in violation of a local ordnance. And deeply hidden in the new healthcare law passed (probably illegally) by Congress in 2010 is a requirement for businesses to file millions more 1099s each year. In other words, I now have to file a Form 1099 for all payees receiving $600 or more per year. Read it for yourself—it's in the law. The IRS will be monitoring this.

And speaking of the IRS, I have had my own problems with that agency. Several years ago, our new bookkeeper misunderstood her responsibilities and failed to pay the 941 taxes for three quarters. She thought our accountant was paying the taxes. The total amount was about $53K. I have since repaid this amount in full, plus $41K in interest and penalties, and still owed the IRS over $100K until late 2015 when the remaining debt was forgiven. Now, because of the Dodd-Frank Wall Street Reform and Consumer Protection Act and the continuing Obama recession, I can't get a reasonable loan anywhere.

In 2012, the Organization for Economic Cooperation and Development (OECD) reported that the US had higher regulatory barriers to new businesses, greater administrative burdens on small businesses, and lower competitive advantages than any other of the industrialized nations.[5] US entrepreneurs face more red tape now than ever before. Because these regulations keep coming at a faster and faster pace, business owners can't predict the scope and impact of new ones. Therefore, they delay buying equipment, restocking merchandise and adding workers.

It gets even worse at the state and local levels. There are additional taxes, license fees, and fines for not complying with the most obscure regulations. The state of Louisiana requires monks to be fully licensed as funeral directors in order to sell their handmade wooden caskets.[6] The city of Philadelphia requires all bloggers to purchase a $300 business license.[7] And in Milwaukee, Wisconsin, in order to go out of business, one must purchase an expensive license, fill out a pile of paperwork, and pay an additional fee for the remaining inventory and any "going out of business" sale.[8]

In my own city of Montgomery, Alabama, I have been threatened with a fine and jail time for putting too many empty boxes out for pickup by the trash detail. And recently the state revenue department informed me that I owed some $44K in sales taxes for the past four years. In Alabama, like other states, schools are tax-exempt entities. We sell a lot of musical instruments and supplies to schools all over the state. These are normally large instruments, like tubas, baritone saxophones, bass clarinets, baritone horns, bass fiddles, tympani, bass drums, etc., that the schools need to fill out their bands and orchestras, as most student musicians' families don't opt to buy these more expensive instruments. This has been the case since we started business in 1955. Then, last year all of a sudden, one of the bureaucrats decided that schools don't buy musical instruments and refigured our tax liability. I am still fighting that one.

It never stops. The bureaucrats have taken over, and they're killing us!

UNIONS

What is the impact of unions in all of this? Over the years they have permeated virtually every part of our economy as well as government. They have merged together under umbrella organizations that are able to exert great pressure to obtain higher and higher salaries and benefits for their members. And because of the tremendous wealth acquired from membership dues, these umbrella organizations (e.g., the AFL-CIO, SEIU, etc.) now have considerable political clout. The private sector hardest hit by the higher personnel costs has been manufacturing, and we have seen many large companies either go out of business or move their plants offshore.

Today, for example, there are no major American manufacturers of musical instruments or sound and recording equipment remaining in operation in the US. Even my good friend, Hartley Peavey, who vowed never to produce his magnificent sound equipment outside the US, has recently gone offshore. His was the last American music company to do this, as far as I know; however, part of his production still remains in the US. Public sector unions have garnered more and more benefits over the years to the point where they are a major reason why a number of state governments are going bankrupt, so both state and federal tax rates are increasing. The effects, of course, trickle down to small businessmen and taxpayers. If our economy is going to recover, the negative impacts that unions are having at all levels of American business and government must be reversed.

This is not to say that the union movement has been all bad. Let's take a brief look at the history of unions in this country. Up through 1870, over half of American laborers worked in agriculture. Aside from agriculture, all kinds of crafts existed, and skilled tradesmen over time began to form craft unions in their specialties. In 1869, the first national labor union was established, which admitted all workers, including farmers and rural shopkeepers. It was called the Knights of Labor and by 1880 had some 700,000 members.[9]

In 1886, Samuel Gompers formed the AFL under the principle of horizontal organization, whereby affiliated national or international craft unions were largely autonomous.[10]   Electricians, for example, could be in the same union regardless of the company they actually worked for. Thus, umbrella labor groups gave greater economic bargaining power to skilled craftsmen than was available to unskilled and semiskilled workers. The AFL essentially superseded the Knights of Labor which disbanded in 1912. Then in 1938, John L. Lewis and several other union leaders formed the CIO to better serve mass-production workers. The new umbrella group was organized on a vertical basis in which workers in the automobile, steel, textile, trucking, rubber, etc., industries were represented by their own separate unions.   Twenty years later (1955), these two umbrella organizations merged to form the AFL-CIO under the leadership of George Meany, although some 55 unions remained independent.[11]

This was indeed an important event in the union movement, and in the mid-20th century, 35% of American workers were union members. In 2010, the AFL-CIO represented an average of 8.5 million workers, while overall union membership totaled 16.1 million or about 12.4% of the

workforce.[12]   One of the oldest affiliates of the AFL-CIO, and
the union that I'm most familiar with, is the American
Federation of Musicians (AFM) which has about 100,000
members. This union was formed in 1896 and by 1906 had
45,000 members. It had a major role in establishing minimum
wages for musicians, supporting the big band era of the
1930s-1950s, and promoting music education and
appreciation in our schools. I became an AFM member in the
1940s when I played the trumpet professionally and toured
with bands throughout the southeast. I credit James C.
Petrillo, the famous AFM president during that time, with the
recognition and respect achieved by professional musicians
both in the US and Canada. For some thirty years (1940-70),
one literally could not play for pay without belonging to the
AFM. After that period, the strength and authority of the
AFM declined to the point where musicians don't necessarily
have to carry a union card in many sections of the country.
For instance, there is no longer a local in Montgomery,
Alabama, and countless other cities. One of my dear friends
toured with the Russ Morgan Orchestra without a union card
for 14+ years (1996-2010).

The AFM in its heyday embodied the main advantages of
the union movement. Working conditions, wages, and benefits
were greatly improved. There are still a pension plan, a
number of insurance options, and various referral programs.
One of the more important features has been the negotiation
of contractual standards for performing musicians across a
wide spectrum of venues—concerts, shows, dances,
recordings, TV, films, commercials, etc. As a result,
musicians realized advances through their bargaining power
as a collective unit. All other unions experienced similar
advances. Wages and benefits increased. Job protection also
became a big advantage of union membership.

On the other hand, unions have been so successful in negotiating generous wage and fringe benefit packages for their members that costs of making American goods are literally out of control in many sectors of the economy. Numerous companies have found themselves unable to compete on US soil as a result. Witness the plight of GM and Chrysler in the 2008-2010 time frame when they were able to stay in business only through the forced largesse of American taxpayers (i.e., government bailouts that resulted in the UAW owning about 40% of GM and 55% of Chrysler and reducing stockholders to minority status[13]). The chief cause? The powerful UAW which had extracted such high wage and benefit concessions and had reduced management flexibility so much that it was impossible for the corporations to be profitable. (Does anybody think the new Chevy Volt is going to be the solution?) Companies that haven't gone under during the current recession have moved their operations to places like China and Southeast Asia where they can realize huge savings in labor costs and thereby continue to be competitive. When all is said and done, businesses (large or small) must make a profit to stay viable and contribute to the economy, i.e., create jobs and provide goods and services.

The one thing that has always puzzled me about unions is this: if forcing higher and higher wages and benefits eventually destroys the company that employs their workers, what ultimate good is that going to do the workers, the union, the company, and even the country? While unions don't directly affect small business nearly as much as they do the large corporation and government, there is an indirect impact in that the wholesale goods and services purchased by small businesses cost more. Neutralization of the negative effects of unions is part of the equation to be solved if our country is going to spring back from the big economic hole it is in.

THE MASS MERCHANDISERS

Here, I am going to repeat a couple of paragraphs from Chapter 3 in case you might have glossed over them, because they set the stage so well for this subject. Again, new rules and regulations relaxing territorial and price protection rang the death knell for many dealers, and the way was then clear for the mass merchandisers and their quantitative discount (QD) system to evolve onto the scene. Slowly at first, and then progressively faster, the public and the mass merchandisers began to find each other.

In my industry, the mass-merchandising discounters' advertisements penetrated the market through direct mailings to the band directors and school officials. Their ads were also in the music magazines and all kinds of other publications, as well as in classified telephone directories listing WATS lines. They achieved virtually 100% penetration of the market. Just about every student had or had access to the discounters' catalogs, and many band directors made the catalogs readily available, often displaying them on their bulletin boards with the exhortation to note the prices and try to get a better price from the local dealer. Respected music merchants, who had spent years in building their reputations for service, integrity, and reliability, suddenly had their positive images questioned and in some cases destroyed. They became the "rip-off dealer" in the eyes of many customers.

I have great respect for the Sam Waltons of the world. They are talented leaders of American business who have been able to take advantage of the system. Walmart has never profited from broken laws. Sam Walton did not do anything wrong. You don't do anything against the law if you take advantage of any legal deductions on your income tax return—not anything legally wrong. However, if you find a loophole that has not been addressed by the courts, you have not broken the law, but have you broken the "spirit of the law?"

Mass merchandising will eventually take over every profession if restraints are not put into place. I don't think that the individuals who initiated the concept of quantity discount (QD) mass merchandising really had any idea of how far they could evolve such a system. It came in little, short steps that were so subtle that hardly anyone recognized what was happening, especially the buying public that was drawn into the system by being baited with purchasing products they needed at cheaper prices. It seems that no one thought it out to see where the system would eventually end. No warning labels were on the boxes, e.g., "WARNING—the use of this system may be hazardous to your country and your personal financial health."

This did not happen overnight. We were essentially lulled to sleep for a while and only now are waking up to a stark reality—our country is in dire economic trouble. And most of the measures being taken at all levels of government seem only to be making matters worse. Once a beacon of hope to the rest of the world, our capitalistic system is under siege and our representative republic is deteriorating. We are totally insane to have let this happen to us.

QD is such an important subject in this context that I am devoting a separate chapter to it in order to provide more detail.

THE INTERNET

Among music dealers in 2011, "the single most talked about issue was the conflict between online and brick-and-mortar retailing. Local retailers, both large and small, are unquestionably feeling the heat from fast-growing online competitors. Their stress is compounded by the fact that they are required to collect sales tax, while their mail order competitors are not. Add that to the still struggling economy, and it's understandable that the mood among traditional retailers is somewhat less than buoyant."[14]

This is one of the most amazing phenomena of my lifetime. I have never been a big fan of computers, because I got along fine without them for so many, many years, but now it is almost impossible to operate a business without them. We have used the AIMsi sales and inventory control system developed by Tri-Tech Solutions in Dubuque, Iowa, for the past 20 years with great success. But with the advent and growth of the Internet, our business has been impacted mostly in negative ways. And now you don't even need a computer to "surf the net"—almost everybody has a Smartphone or iPhone that affords instant access to any Internet site. In the current environment, most traditional retailers like me are no longer able to maintain large inventories on hand and therefore often cannot compete well with on-line venues.

First of all, more quantity discount houses have emerged on the Internet, such as the Woodwind & Brasswind, Guitar Center, Best Buy, etc., that are selling new musical instruments for about the same price that we have to pay for them. For example, just as soon as I quote my best price on a brand new Yanagisawa tenor saxophone, the customer is already looking at one on his cell phone for a cheaper price. All of the "big box" stores have their own web sites. Moreover, most of their customers don't have to pay sales tax. Shipping charges normally apply, but many sellers offer free shipping. We have to pay shipping and handling charges on anything we order from our wholesalers.

Secondly, the auction sites, like eBay and Amazon, provide a ready venue for the purchase of second hand instruments at very attractive prices. This has a horrible effect on our used instrument sales and rentals. School band and orchestra directors are encouraging their students to look for bargains on-line instead of recommending local dealers. Unfortunately, some of these bargains are junk and impossible to maintain in playing condition.

Thirdly, the Internet now provides the variety of options in instruments and accessories that we once could offer because loans were available for us to stock our shelves for the new school year. As noted earlier, the loans have dried up, and we can no longer do this. Consumers would rather purchase on-line where they can readily make their choices rather than pay extra for a special order at the music store.

Yes, we have developed our own web site and have listed items for sale on-line, but more often than not our prices are not competitive due to our higher wholesale costs. While online selling may be the hottest market segment going today, there's no guarantee that an online presence will be successful.[15] All things considered, the Internet has not been advantageous for us. This may be at least partially attributable to ". . . Digital Darwinism, . . . when technology and society are evolving faster that the ability of many organizations to adapt."[16]

PS: Al Gore did NOT invent the Internet.

Chapter 5

EVOLVEMENT OF THE QUANTITY DISCOUNT (QD)

According to the SBA, small businesses make up 99.7% of US employer firms.[1] One can find a variety of statistics on the survival rate of these businesses. I have read or heard somewhere that eight out of ten new businesses fail in their first year. About half survive beyond five years, and about a third make it past ten years. All I know is what I see when I drive through almost any city in the US—small store after small store closed, their buildings vacant and boarded up. And nearby, in too many cases, there'll be one or more big box stores—quantity discount (QD) merchandisers—with full parking lots. I have personally experienced the demise of small businesses losing the ability to be profitable. I know what I am talking about because I have lived through and experienced all of this. What is happening now is just the tip of the iceberg to where it is headed. We must wake up before it is too late to salvage our economy.

In 2004, there were some 24 million small businesses in the United States. There was a growth of 7.3% in proprietors' income, while business bankruptcies fell by 2.1%, and self-employment rose by 2.2%.[2] Since then, these numbers have taken a turn for the worse. The rise of the quantity discount mass merchants (and the Internet) has taken a heavy toll. Little by little, they have taken away the ability of small business—the little guy—to compete. There is a lot of potential in the little guys in the marketplace; they just need a level playing field.

I am writing this section on a Saturday night, having spent most of the previous week in negotiations for the purchase of a failed music store, one of the largest in the southeast. Somehow over the years I have developed the reputation for buying out other music stores that are going out of business. This was the 34th such store that I have purchased. You probably have no idea of the depressing emotions one feels when taking over the assets of a store that is no longer going to remain in business. At one time this store was one of the leading music outlets in the south. With a 24,000-square-foot, state-of-the-art facility, they moved millions and millions of dollars of merchandise over the life of the business. It was a well-managed, family business that was successful because of good service and dedication of the owners. Many of the employees have spent most of their lives working at the store along with the second and third generations of the founder's family. The store is located in a major metropolitan city. How could such a successful store suffer such a demise?

There were seven factors that prevented the family business from sustaining a viable profit margin:

1. Two large, super rich quantity discount music houses came into the city.
2. The owner felt compelled to compete with their heavily discounted prices.
3. The two new super stores were not paying their employees all that much, while the family-owned business had increased salaries over the years.
4. In addition to the two new music discount stores, other area mass merchandise department stores had begun to sell musical instruments (made mostly in China, Taiwan, and India) at cutthroat prices.

5. Many people also were beginning to buy musical instruments on the Internet at discount prices and not having to pay a sales tax.

6. Because of their large quantity purchases, the mass merchandisers could negotiate much cheaper prices from their wholesalers, prices not available to the smaller family business.

7. This left only accessory items and slow-moving specialty items not carried by the discount houses for the family business to rely on for its sales.

One of the reasons this was such a great store was the fact that it stocked almost everything musical. The owners were willing to make this investment to maintain their customer base, and for many years they were able to realize a reasonable profit. They characteristically went "above and beyond" to promote music education and provide repair and technical service in the area of the country that they served. This is pretty much the same policy I have applied in my business. Once the discount houses and the Internet moved into the picture, competition dictated that they sell their products at or below cost. No entity, except perhaps for government, can operate under such circumstances. What happened to this great store has happened and is happening again and again to all types of small retailers in America.

There is a noteworthy aside to be taken from this story, and that is the very positive attitude of the store owner from whom I bought this business. What happened to him would totally devastate most individuals. His positive outlook exemplifies the way he views all of life. He is looking forward to the future and not looking back at the past. We can all learn a valuable lesson from him.

BACKGROUND

One trade magazine editor traces it all back to Henry Ford, whose mass production processes made the automobile accessible to all. "Indirectly, he [Ford] can also take credit (or blame, depending on your point of view) for the shopping mall, the supermarket, big box stores, and most of the other retail formats that currently dot the landscape. None would have been possible without the mobility afforded by the car."[3] But as far as I can determine, Henry Ford cannot be credited with the creation of quantity discounting. It was back in the late 19th century when the mass-marketing revolution began, facilitated mainly by the railroads. They offered mass distribution, and the manufacturers contributed national advertising campaigns, set up exclusive territorial rights for their products, and established minimum retail prices (MRSPs).[4]

The Great Atlantic and Pacific Tea Company (A&P) was founded near the start of the Civil War. It developed its own brand of tea and sold it at discount prices by mail. Later its tea shops stocked spices, baking powder, and canned goods, and it soon became one of the first grocery chains. It was the largest retailer in the world by 1920, ultimately comprising some 16,000 stores. A&P was the Walmart of its day. Customers loved the stores and the prices, but the small grocers and grocery wholesalers had differing views. More than half of the states levied heavy taxes on A&P. The federal government investigated the giant for some 25 years. The American Fair Trade League urged the passage of state laws prohibiting retail price-cutting. Yet, A&P lived on for many, many years. (I had high school friends who worked as bagboys there.) But in the 1950s, restraints on discount retailing, chain-store taxes, and state laws protecting small businesses faded away.[5]

So QD is certainly not new, but QD as a problem for today's small businesses is a fairly recent phenomenon. It all started in 1962 when Sam Walton opened his first Walmart store in Benton County, Arkansas, where a century earlier (1862) the pivotal Battle of Pea Ridge was fought.[6] (These two events are unrelated, but as I have pointed out, one of the purposes of this book is to educate the reader.) The Confederate Army lost that battle, but Sam Walton a century later embarked on his own civil war in retailing, and today his Walmarts and Sam's Clubs constitute the world's greatest retail enterprise. As one author put it, Walton did it by "pummeling hapless American competitors" through a well-crafted strategy and a new business format.[7]

Ranking at the top of the Fortune 500, "Walmart sets the standards and controls its own destiny in every retail area. It makes the retail competition rules, and can change them whenever it likes. And what everyone else is learning is that it's virtually impossible to hold your own in a competition when the rules of engagement are set by the largest, strongest, and fastest competitor."[8] In a nutshell, Sam Walton implemented a most successful rural-retailing discount strategy with his "low price, stack it high, and let it fly" merchandising tactics.[9]

The first big box store of any consequence that I remember coming to Montgomery, Alabama, was K-Mart. That was back in the mid-1970s, and the store thrived for a number of years. Then the first Walmart arrived in 1985, apparently with a better QD system, and at the turn of the new century, the K-Mart store and its "Blue Light Specials" had vanished. In the 1980s we had a Home Quarters Warehouse that had great success in the home improvement arena before later yielding to Home Depot and Lowe's. Home Quarters came to an end, not because it was a bad operation, but because its parent company, Hechinger, went bankrupt. (This was before anybody in our government dreamed up the bad idea of bailouts.) Anyway, fast forward to 2016, and now we have four Walmart Super Centers, two Walmart Neighborhood Markets, a Sam's Club Warehouse, and a Costco in Montgomery, not to mention other Walmarts in nearby Prattville and Wetumpka. This is a pattern witnessed by many cities across our fruited plains.

Too many years ago, when I studied economics and marketing, there were several ways of organizing for business. One, of course, was the stand-alone retailer, which described most small businesses—the mom-and-pop stores. Another was called horizontal integration, where a single company operates a number of different, but often related, businesses. A good example is GM with its Cadillac, Buick, Chevrolet, and GMC (and not too long ago its Oldsmobile and Pontiac) divisions. Then, there was vertical integration, an arrangement where one company or corporation owns all or most of the supply chain of a product or service, from its production to its final sale to consumers. Lowe's, for instance, markets its own line of Task Force products (made in China) that are prominent in their retail outlets. Another example is the Apple Corporation, which is organized on the basis of controlling its products from manufacture to end sale, a clear-cut application of the vertical integration strategy.

In reality, the distinctions between these definitions are somewhat blurred, as most larger companies reflect a combination of these organizational strategies. More recently, management schools began to teach a number of "new" concepts of business and marketing design, such as functional or U-Form, conglomerate or H-Form, divisional or M-Form, matrix, and hybrid.[10] Simply put, business approaches can be categorized in a variety of ways, depending on managerial decisions regarding how best to tailor operations for optimal profit. That's about all we need to say about this, as you can delve further into this subject on your own if desired.

HOW QD GAINED ITS FOOTHOLD

Okay, here goes. Manufacturers each year publish price lists and send them out to all of the dealers. These are called "confidential price lists," and they are not to be revealed to consumers. I'll not elaborate more on the confidentiality aspect here, as I'm devoting a full chapter to it later. Suffice it to say that these price lists provide a suggested retail price on each and every product plus a discount schedule for different quantity levels that might be purchased by the dealer. The lists also establish minimum annual sales volumes in order for a dealer to remain an authorized outlet and are often applicable to a specified geographical zone.

There were always quantity discounts, at least from the time I went into business in 1955. But there is a big difference between then and now. Probably the most relevant factor bearing on what has become destructive QD in the last 60 or so years has been the gradual, insidious increase in the level of inflation. The cumulative rate of inflation has been 790.5%, and it takes $8.90 today to buy a dollar's worth of goods in 1955.[11] So if a top-of-the-line Selmer (Mark XI) alto saxophone sold for $350-$500 in 1955, it would cost approximately $3150-$4500 today. Yet, recent pricing by Conn-Selmer shows a minimum advertised price (MAP) well above that, i.e., $6519 for a Reference 54-Spirit of Mark VI model.[12] Obviously, there is more of an exponential, rather than a simple, straight line, relationship between inflation and prices, especially over the last 30 years.

Let's examine this further. What made the American economy in the 1980s so ready for the mass merchandise discounters, the big box stores? In comparison to 1955, we saw a rise in consumer prices across the board due principally to inflation and a rise in production costs as labor union pressure brought about progressively higher wages and benefits. (See Chapter 4 for more on unions.) The average rate of inflation in 1955 was -0.28%—for all practical purposes 0%—which makes 1955 almost a perfect base year to begin our analysis.[13] This means essentially that one US dollar ($1) was actually worth one US dollar ($1), something we're not likely to see ever again. Moreover, prices were relatively stable throughout much of the 1950s. Since 1957, the average core inflation rate has been 3.72% annually.[14] Core inflation is normally based on a chosen measure, like the Consumer Price Index (CPI), that excludes the more volatile factors of food and energy prices. By 1985, the cumulative rate of inflation reached 301.5%, and it took $4 to buy what had cost only $1 in 1955.[15]

In 1955, you could buy a nice house for $22,000, the latest Ford automobile for $1606-$2944, a first class postage stamp for 3 cents, a dozen eggs for 61 cents, a loaf of bread for 18 cents, and a gallon of gasoline for 23 cents. Average annual income was $4,137.[16] In the music business, a top-of-the-line Selmer alto saxophone ran about $500. This would have been the new Mark VI introduced in 1954 or the Balanced Action that had been around a while and was still the preferred model in my store as well as stores across the country. A Selmer Centered Tone clarinet, one of the models played by Benny Goodman, sold for $180-$200. These price ranges were pretty much the same for most all of the extant brands of the day—Conn, King, Blessing, Leblanc, Boosey & Hawkes, Buescher, Gemeinhardt, Holton, Olds, Martin, Besson, Bundy, Bach, Buffet Campon, etc.

By 1985, Ford prices ranged from $6,000 to $14,000, depending on which of many models one selected.[17] The average cost of buying a house was between $40,000 and $89,330, the latter price being for a new, high end dwelling, and the average income per year was $22,100. A gallon of gasoline was $1.20, a first class postage stamp had gone up to 22 cents, a loaf of bread to 74 cents, and a dozen eggs to 80 cents. Incidentally, the national debt was only $1,817.5B back then.[18] It's anybody's guess as to how long it might take us to get it down to that level again, that is if we ever can get started. Many pundits and "talking heads" say it's not even possible.

By 1985, in the musical instrument industry the Producer Price Index (PPI) rose to 100, indicating that the cost of making and distributing instruments was at least twice as much as it was in 1955.[19] PPI is a key factor in determining the reasons for changes in the CPI, although factors other than inflation may also bear upon retail price increases.[20] Accordingly, retail prices rose also. A Selmer Mark VI alto saxophone now ran $1500-$1800, and a top Selmer clarinet, Series 9 or 10, was $700-$1000. The Buffet R13 clarinet was $900-$1200. The Blessing ML-1 Artist trumpet was selling for about $660, its B-155 Artist flugelhorn about $745, its B-98 bass trombone about $1675, and its B-450 tuba around $2475.[21] All prices for woodwinds and brass instruments were substantially higher across the board. Prices for virtually all goods and services had increased quite a bit over the preceding 30 years.

It was about this time that I saw the need for a trumpet (remember that I had been a professional trumpet player for years) that would be considered in the professional line (like the Bach Stradivarius) but within the price range of a student.[22] Randy Johnson of the Blessing Company agreed to produce the trumpet, and I began selling them in 1986 for $575. Since then, thousands of these Model 45 Darby trumpets have been sold. "The horn is silver plated, has a first valve saddle, stop rod and nut on the third valve slide (like a Bach). In fact, bracing and the two posts on the leadpipe and tuning slide [are designed] like a Strad."[23] Today the Darby trumpet remains a bargain at under $800.[24]

So the stage was set for Walmart, and its "We Sell for Less" slogan, and other mass merchandisers to take advantage of the economic environment that existed back then and attract customers who wanted lower prices. They gained rapid popularity because they carried huge inventories and offered those lower prices. The method they used to do this was deep quantity discounting in their wholesale purchasing of products, discounts far more than those normally given to traditional retailers. Since then, inflation has continued to climb. PPI is now 214.1; general costs of production have more than tripled since 1955.[25] Retail prices have sky-rocketed (along with the national debt), and the big box stores are as popular as ever. They appear here to stay.

We have evolved into a system (QD) where you cannot get ahead with hard work and perseverance. Because of QD our American free enterprise system no longer is workable, making the American dream just about unobtainable any more in traditional industries. Our American population, every man, woman, and child in America, needs to be educated as to how our business system works and the advantages that accrue when that system is successful and profitable. When the system is right, then hard work, perseverance, endurance, and dedication will ensure success. Under the QD system, success is in direct proportion to how much money (financial resources) you have, which perpetuates the rich becoming richer and more powerful, and perpetuates the poor staying poor.

THE IMPACT

As I have noted earlier, I am brick and mortar. Brick and mortar stores can do things for the public that no other entities can do. I can't speak for every business, but my store is well known for going above and beyond in serving its customers. This is part of what I do and my store does for the public. How many big box stores can say that they provide this kind of service?

Visualize our America without brick and mortar. Theoretically, it's easy to do all of your shopping under one roof—save gas, save time, big selection and low prices, quick checkout (maybe)—where all too often product specifications are set to lower levels of quality by the mass merchandiser. For example, go ahead and buy your foreign-made band instrument at a heavily discounted price, and then try to send it back to the manufacturer or service center if you have trouble. Good luck!

I have to say that "Made in America" does not carry the clout that it once did. At one time, it meant that you could not buy anything better . . . it was well worth the price even if you might have to pay more for the product. It was made to exacting standards by people who took great pride in their work and their company. The expertise of their workmanship, the superior design, and lasting quality were built into the product. In their quest for cheap products, the QD mass merchants have been a major player in causing the virtual end of traditional "Made in America" quality, work ethic and skill levels, not to mention small business.

I don't think that the individuals who initiated the concept of QD mass merchandising really had any idea of how far that they could develop this type of merchandising. It came in little, short steps that were so subtle that hardly anyone recognized what was happening . . . especially the buying public that was drawn into the system by being baited with purchasing the products that they needed at cheaper prices. In my own business, there have always been volume discounts built into the manufacturers' price structures, but they always seemed reasonable and conducive to business success—until recent years. It seems that no one thought it out to see where the system would eventually end. No warning labels were on the boxes: "WARNING: The use of this system may be hazardous to your country and your personal financial health."

Consider the distress of service-oriented businesses, which are devastated and destroyed because the super rich QD merchants are able to beat the manufacturer down in price so that no one can compete with them. Just think about those brave and noble souls who go into business, work long and hard to make the business successful in serving the public, then to have their business devastated through no fault of their own. Thousands and thousands of both new and long established retailers are being forced into bankruptcy—forced to sell or liquidate their businesses for pennies on the dollar. We must put a stop to this devastation. We can't allow it to continue to destroy the business community, the families, and the very economic fabric of American society. Who has been looking out for the working American people? No one!

Quantity discounters have crept in, and the result is the vilest type of discrimination, robbing our children of their God-given freedoms. It is a system that keeps the poor, poor and the rich, rich. Yet, you never hear anything about this inhumane form of economic discrimination. Today, with the quantity discount (QD) system, we have an almost impossible business situation. Our business universities and financial advisors admonish us not to carry any more merchandise than necessary to make the sale, but the system forces us to take excess inventory and bear the costs of storage, obsolescence (e.g., electronics, produce, clothing styles, etc.), interest and finance charges, insurance, and loss due to the inability to take cash discounts. The mental pressures of all of this destroy the fundamental incentives to want to be in business. Being in business today has evolved into a form of warfare.

QD is responsible for the value of all of your consumer goods (your assets) dropping in value. If you are in business and have accumulated an inventory, it goes down in value, and cost of government continues to go up. In order to keep costs down, many times the big box stores require the quality specifications to be scaled down to sell at cheaper prices.

Bigger is not necessarily better. When a new QD store opens, they initially man the store with more personnel; then they cut back the number of personnel almost down to a skeleton crew once they're established. I shopped in Montgomery's latest Walmart and the new Costco just after they opened. At that time, every one of their 14-26 cashier lanes were manned. Now it's rare to find open more than three lanes. Maybe their pricing is good, but the service is bad. Many times it is hard for customers in a mass merchandise store to even locate the item they are looking for, not to mention practical information about the product or service. It is most unusual to find a really knowledgeable employee in mass merchandising. If they are knowledgeable, it probably is because they previously worked in a brick and mortar small business.

In a large sense, small dealers subsidize the big box dealers. If it were not for all of the many sales that a manufacturer makes to the smaller dealers, the manufacturer would not be able to cut the prices lower for the mass merchandiser. A large portion of the manufacturers will not be honest about this, and it makes it hard for the manufacturers' representatives to attempt to convince the small dealer (often lying to him) that the mass merchandiser is paying the same wholesale price that the small dealer is charged.

Because of QD and the erosion of profitability, a large percentage of manufacturers, jobbers, and distributors (not to mention retailers) have been forced to cut back or completely eliminate their outside (traveling) sales personnel. There's just not enough profit to justify the expense unless the sales personnel have the expertise and initiative to create new business. When the manufacturer's representative (rep) stops calling on the dealer and the dealer, without rep attention, slows down or gradually stops buying from the non-represented manufacturer, supply lines and sales dry up. As profitability decreases, banking relationships erode...who wants to loan you money in today's economy? This is totally disruptive to an effective, vibrant capitalistic system, one that we ought to be able to rely on to pull us out of the present economic slump.

I'll bet that the typical small business owner feels slighted when he sees what exorbitant compensation that many of the CEOs of American companies are making. True, if the CEO has his money invested in the business, he has the right to expect a return on his investment over and above his duties and responsibilities in the company. If you had bought stock in Coca-Cola in 1945 and you decide to sell that stock today, you certainly would not want to sell it at the same price you paid for that stock in 1945. You are entitled to have a return on your investment. But the huge compensation package of many top CEOs is inimical to the morale of the middle class business owner who is struggling to make all of his financial ends meet.

It is often observed that America is no longer a primary industrial or manufacturing nation. In fact, manufacturing remains the dominant industry in only seven US states. We are fast becoming a service economy, with the health care and social assistance industries now the largest employers in 34 states.[26] But there is no way that we can sustain our economy and standard of living just as a service-oriented economy. For a short time, we might think it is working, but not for long.

In the music industry two of our companies, Fender and Bose, opened plants in Mexico in the 1990s to make amplification and audio products at prices far under everyone else. Fender also moved its guitar manufacturing facilities to Japan, Mexico, China, and Korea, while closing down those facilities in the US.[27] Of course, when this happened, it compelled competing companies, except for Peavey (see Chapter 7 for more on Peavey), to go to off-shore also and do the same thing. Not only did this cause our American workers to lose their jobs in manufacturing, but these low prices spawned other problems. The retail price to the consumer was so low that it became unreasonable to pay the American service technician to repair the units. So more pollution to the planet occurs as the unit is pitched into the trash rather than being repaired. This is the same thing that has happened with many other electronic items in your home and business. All of these products are made of materials that came out of the ground (Earth's resources, like silver, etc.), and it is far better for our planet to do the repairs rather than discard the products. We are trashing ourselves into a lower level of existence rather than conserving our precious, non-renewable resources.

QD impacts every facet of life in America. Should you think that this book might just be a scare tactic, then just look at the facts—the national debt, the negative balance of trade with foreign nations, the mass exodus of manufacturing from our country, the business failure rate. QD has played a major role in all of these trends.

Let's suppose that you are a huge (QD) national or global retailer, and let's suppose that I am a manufacturer. This year, I manufacture a product that I sell to you for $100.00. In order to continue to sell my product in your stores, you force me to agree to put things in place so that I can sell you the identical model product for $95.00 next year. In order to continue selling my product in your stores, I have to agree to drop the price 5% each year from the price the year before. Eventually the QD retailer either destroys me, owns me, and/or forces me to shut down manufacturing in the US and go off-shore where I can get cheap labor to build the product.

Just because I drop my price each year does not necessarily mean that the mass merchandiser drops the price to the consumer. As long as the public continues to buy the product at the existing price, the excess profit is probably just added to the mass merchant's bottom line net profit. Nonetheless, when the manufacturers shut down or curtail manufacturing in America, then production workers lose their jobs and the trickle-down effect damages the economy in a long range, devastating manner.

QD is a deceptive monster that kills the opportunity for success. You may struggle for years and years to grow a business to the size to be able to get "over the hump" to where you can buy at top discount levels. Yet if you have great wealth you could open a business and be able to immediately get maximum quantity discounts so as to almost immediately be able to destroy all of your smaller dealers. To me, this is not a "civilized" concept. QD takes money out of the economy and destroys manufacturers, distributors, and retailers alike. How can you pay a decent salary to your employees when the gross profit is not there? There has to be a profit motivation in business—although there is a great thrill, feeling, and intrinsic reward to be had in building a business where service is the key, not your ability to buy in quantity.

American manufactures are being beat down to unprofitability by super stores, buying groups, big box stores, Internet, and catalog operations to the place that they have been forced to curtail or shut down. They are forced to go off-shore if they are going to survive. This is just a prelude for the storm to come.

It is very hard for the small dealer to be profitable today. Many times, the retailer literally serves as a showroom for the shopper to see, try, and inspect the merchandise but cannot make the sale. "Music stores are one of the last specialty retailers in business. . .. Now the nails are being pounded into the local music stores' coffin [sic] by mail order, internet [sic], manufacturer pricing policies, and taxes. . . . Mail order companies offer free freight, no taxes, and 30 days to look at the merchandise, and map [sic] prices everyday [sic]."[28] In my area we have to collect a 10% sales tax. That puts my local music store at a 10% price disadvantage from the get-go. The price printed on the price sheet from your supplier is not etched in stone by any stretch of the imagination. Small mom-and-pop stores such as mine are actually subsidizing the QD super stores by paying higher wholesale prices than those larger stores.[29]

"The new MAP prices are hurting the small store as MAP pricing has become the retail price. You can no longer place a retail price on an instrument and expect not to come down to map [sic] price if you want to sell the instrument. Just about any kid who comes in your front door already knows the MAP price and expects to buy at the MAP price or at a lower price because yours has some light marks on the instrument from customer's [sic] trying out the instrument in your shop.

"We work hard to present the manufacturers' merchandise so that the shopper can view it only for the shopper to go home to mail order it over his computer. What does the manufacturer do for the local guy? Nothing. But they give the big guy an advertising allowance that we as small dealers would never receive. Manufacturers will sometime[s] hold out a carrot for the small store, but when we try to grab it, it will be just out of reach. I remember when the music business was profitable for the small guy. Today, I feel more like I work for the government."[30]

I would like to see a study of what happens to the profits (i.e., follow the money) made by mass and Internet merchandisers. Is it coming back into the economy? I suspect not as much as we might hope! Our country's economy has basically been built by small business. Only in comparatively recent times has this begun to change. Small business spends money and hires employees who also spend money— most of what they take in almost immediately goes back into the economy. I do not believe it is the same with many of the QD mass merchandisers. Their heavy profits are in large measure not coming back into the economy, and much of their earnings may even be going off-shore into foreign banks and foreign economies.

Chapter 6

BUSINESS SECRETS YOU NEED TO KNOW ABOUT

This is probably the most frustrating issue of all to a local dealer who has spent a lifetime serving the public, especially our young, school-aged musicians. One of the purposes of this book is to present an exposé by a "Top 50 in America" music dealer—to tell the public about the secrets that are destroying the country's economy in a racketeering manner.

Because of confidential price lists developed by the various manufacturers and jobbers (middlemen), I am unable to purchase musical instruments at the same price as the QD merchandisers. The wholesale prices vary for each retailer based on quantity levels, in terms of both product volume and the amount of money involved.

When I started my music store in 1955, business relationships were simpler, more straightforward. Various manufacturers and craftsmen produced the musical instruments we carried. At that time, some of the very best instruments were made in Paris, France, and some were made in Elkhart and Elkhorn, Indiana. These instruments were distributed by jobbers or wholesalers, who represented the manufacturer or who purchased the instruments for further distribution to retailers across the country. The manufacturers set the wholesale price based on the costs of making and shipping the instruments plus a reasonable profit. The manufacturers would also provide a suggested retail price as a guideline for both jobbers and retailers. The jobbers then added a reasonable mark-up to cover their costs and make a profit. Finally the dealers or retailers would apply the suggested retail price, which covered the wholesale and shipping costs and assured a reasonable profit. Retailers all paid pretty much the same wholesale prices to stock their stores.

Dealers additionally were granted geographic territories in which to market certain brand names. For example, for years my store had the rights to market Selmer band and orchestra instruments in Alabama. Later, one of our competitors held the rights for Yamaha instruments. This is the way it worked, and it worked very well for all concerned.

But it all began to unravel some thirty years ago with the advent of the big box stores, the QD mass merchandisers. Wholesale prices over time became something less than straightforward and common knowledge, and big volume retailers began to receive preferential pricing that wasn't available to smaller retailers. Moreover, cash discounts and rebates for volume purchases became widespread, further complicating the lives of small businessmen. Today, ". . .it seems impossible to compete directly with big-box retailers like Wal-mart [sic] on price . . . ! The combination of their buying power of big brands, private-label programs, off-shore manufacturing, distribution efficiencies, culture, expense structure, company-owned truck fleet, and low-paying non-union jobs provide[s] a vise-like grip on costs no competitor can match."[1]

But that's not all there is to it. The price lists are being kept confidential so that no small retailer can be sure whether he is getting a good wholesale price or not. As noted in the previous chapter, confidential dealer discounts have long been used to keep American citizens—the consumers—from knowing what is going on. What once was open knowledge to retailers is now close-hold, depending on which retailer is being dealt with. Manufacturers and wholesalers are making separate, secret deals with different dealers, and now even directly with consumers mainly through the Internet. The prices and discounts vary so greatly that, except for the mass merchandisers who are getting the lower prices, most retailers cannot plan their inventories with any confidence that they can turn a profit. Frankly, I don't know how the manufacturers and wholesalers manage to keep up with so many different price structures. I've already said it makes MY head spin.

Then there's MAP (minimum advertised price) pricing that has come into the picture. This is also a relatively new development, and it's not the same as the old manufacturer's suggested retail price. This means that the latter can no longer be used as before because the MAP is normally quite a bit lower. "Few terms in the [music] industry evoke as much emotion as this acronym."[2] The MAP prices are now part of the confidential listings, and they exacerbate the volatility and impact of those listings by reducing any flexibility the small dealer might have in favorably setting his own prices. "If a small, brick-and-mortar combo store represents 12 manufacturers, the store has 12 different MAP policies to follow."[3] You almost have to hire a pricing specialist to keep up with all of these variations. This is further compounded by the fact that manufacturers are constantly releasing updated price lists all during the year.[4] And what makes it a real nightmare is having to update the computer data base and re-price the inventory every time these changes occur.

BACKGROUND

From its beginning, America has been a capitalistic society. Tradesmen, merchants, farmers, ranchers, etc., all depended on some form of profit, whether in kind, bartered exchange, or currency. Otherwise, why bother? With the onset of WWI, America's Industrial Revolution began, when mechanization of production—or mass production—literally changed the landscape of the western world. The American industrial system was summed up "as the production, for private profit, of more and more goods at lower costs and the increased distribution of these goods at lower prices."[5]

It was out of this era that emerged the idea of the confidential price lists. Every level of the system knew instinctively that profit drove the engine of the American economy. The result was the creation of a standard of living and opportunity for an entire population that had never before been achieved in the history of mankind. And today the US still represents the prevailing beacon of hope for humanity, while at the same time malevolent forces, both within and without, continue to try to tear her down.

Over time, manufacturers in all sectors of the economy published price lists that considered a number of important factors. First, of course, would be the production costs and the amount of profit required by the manufacturer. Then, the distribution costs and a profit for the jobber were calculated. Finally, the retailer's costs (basically the wholesale price and shipping), plus a reasonable profit rounded out the equation. The determining rationale was that the final sale to the consumer was crucial to the success of the entire chain of events. In other words, if the retailer could not profit from the sale of the product, the manufacturer and jobber would soon be out of business. In the most basic sense, profit is essential to everything in our lives.

CONFIDENTIALITY EXPOSED

Years ago, our predecessors in business must have felt like their customers did not have sufficient maturity to comprehend that there has to be a built-in percentage of profit in order for a retail establishment to realize enough gross revenue to pay expenses and invest further in the operation. Back then, they were probably right. Experienced retailers knew it, but they kept the details hidden from the customers.

Early consumers paid the stated price for items they needed without giving too much thought to how much profit was being accrued by the merchant or store owner. Even today, most of the public that has never run a retail establishment has little knowledge of what profit margin is mandatory for a business to be viable.

Without a sufficient amount of profit, a business cannot possibly succeed. Most anyone who has been in business for any length of time knows this. By the same token, competition dictates that a business cannot expect to make enormous profits but must be satisfied with reasonable earnings. Historically, the confidential price lists provided to the retailers were fairly standard and equitable; they allowed the retailers enough latitude to compete and determine their own profit margin as best suited their businesses. It seemed logical not to reveal to the public anything concerning what percentage of the sale price would constitute profit, and there were no efforts to educate the general public. The system was set up on the basis of secrecy between the supplier and dealer. Under no circumstances was a dealer to show the confidential discount schedule to a customer. Any violation of this confidentiality could mean withdrawal of dealership privileges by the manufacturer.

Now that the mass merchandisers have all but taken over, and QD is so prevalent, the confidential price lists are doing more harm than good to small businesses. Today, the traditional retailers can't find out what kinds of secret deals are being made with the big box stores; all they know is that they can't get those same deals. Even the big box stores don't know what kinds of deals other big box stores are getting. And the big box merchandisers with their "sell for less" slogans aren't about to reveal their profit levels. I'm not sure the FBI could figure it all out. But I feel like I have an obligation to tell it like it is.

Okay, here goes. Manufacturers each year publish price lists and send them out to all of the dealers. These are called "confidential price lists," and they are not to be revealed to consumers. These price lists provide a suggested retail price on each and every product plus a discount schedule for different quantity levels that might be purchased by the dealer. The lists also establish minimum annual sales volumes in order for a dealer to remain an authorized outlet and are often applicable to a specified geographical zone.

These publications contain a detailed description of something called a master order program. Master orders are arranged in different groups with a number of levels in each group. In the music industry, for example, Leblanc in 1993 specified certain band and orchestra instruments to constitute Group I and others to constitute Group II. Student instruments were in Group I, and intermediate and professional instruments were in Group II. Master orders for each group were described in terms of volume discount level and the calendar date of the order. Orders below a certain volume were not considered to be master orders. The base discount for Group I was 50%, but if master orders were placed, the dealer could take an additional discount of 5-15%, depending on the number of units ordered. And if the order were placed by the end of February, a further 15% discount was possible—for a total of 80%. To qualify for a master order, Leblanc dealers had to purchase 30 or more units in Group I or II. But wait—that's not all! Leblanc also offered extended credit, special cash discounts, and end-of-year rebates.[6]

Is your head spinning yet? Mine sure is, and I've been wrestling with these price lists for 60+ years. To further complicate matters, Conn-Selmer in 2012 departed from its exclusive distribution system through retail dealers and began to market designated instruments through the Internet and dealer affiliates. This essentially meant that

Conn-Selmer had decided to operate in direct competition with its dealers. They also announced the adoption of a unilateral Minimum Advertised Price (MAP) policy for all of their dealers. Accordingly, instruments and accessories covered by this policy could not be advertised for less than the MAP shown in the price list.[7]

So now the price lists include both a suggested retail price (MSRP) and a MAP price. Ostensibly, the MAP is supposed to enable manufacturers and dealers to receive adequate profits, but in most cases the MAP prices are about 30% lower than the MSRPs. While well intentioned, MAP prices are often murky and contradictory. "There exists no consistent MAP policy for our [music] industry. As a result, each manufacturer makes up its own policy, enforcement methods and standard of what constitutes compliance."[8] The whole thing is so confusing that I don't know how anybody can keep up with it today. And each manufacturer has its own unique set of price lists.

Moreover, the rules for applying MAP prices have some gaping holes in them. We have Internet retailers listing items for less than the MAP, using the "open box" dodge. Ostensibly, this implies that the item is not brand new, even though it is being advertised as new, and therefore can be sold below the MAP. The "display model" and "demo item" are other dodges used to get around the pricing requirements, loopholes that frustrate the small dealer trying to maintain a legitimate business.[9] I've also seen new items being sold as factory "seconds," the defacing of an item in order to discount it, the waiver of fake insurance, and the free freight loophole.

What's really devastating to the small dealer goes well beyond all of this—it's the quantity discounts to the mass merchandisers that aren't in the published "confidential price lists." Every big-box retailer now can make special deals with manufacturers, and nobody else knows what they are. This under-the-table practice basically nullifies every arrangement that traditionally worked to the advantage of all concerned, including the small retailer. But QD has all but cut small dealers out of the pattern. All I know is that the Woodwind & Brasswind, Musician's Friend, Guitar Center, etc., can sell new instruments for less than my wholesale price from the manufacturer or jobber, and that I'm not allowed to buy at the same wholesale price as those big boxers. This is because I cannot possibly order in sufficient volumes to reach down to the same wholesale price levels and discounts and other considerations given to the mass merchandisers. Even if I formed a buying group with the two other privately-owned music stores in Montgomery, it would still be impossible. Small retailers like me are at a competitive disadvantage, and that's the main reason so many have failed and are failing across the nation. And, of course, it's not just music stores that are affected—virtually all small businesses are suffering. This evolution happened so gradually, almost imperceptibly, that nobody really noticed the "discount creep" until it took its toll.

SHOULD THIS SECRECY CONTINUE?

This book is designed to promote honesty and openness. It is designed to kill dealer dishonesty and deception. It is designed to kill confidentiality. It is designed to make business honest. It is designed to restore good will between manufacturer, distributor, retailer and the retailer's customers.

If the public has been deceived into supporting a corrupt system that they did not realize they were supporting, then that system needs to be exposed. The QD mass merchants have quietly and cleverly kept the knowledge of this away from public view so that very few people know what is going on. In the trade, it is known as confidential dealer discounts;

it is to be kept secret. The public must be educated as to what has been kept secret from them so that they then can do something to stop the deception, corruption, and destruction of our nation's businesses, and ultimately the destruction of our country.

We have all heard the adage that "you cannot legislate morality." Possibly this could be true. However, we can create a set of just and fair rules that, if obeyed, would be designed to protect us from being harmed by others who might have lost their moral perspective—those who have created retailing monsters that are so powerful that they can cripple, incapacitate, destroy or kill other competing retailers that do not have as much QD purchasing power.

The people who own these retail giants possibly have lost their compassion and concern for those whom they destroy, but they still need to understand the implications of what they are doing beyond their own profit. Just as manufacturers must not force dealers to buy more than the dealer can sell or pay for, the QD merchants should not be forcing manufacturers to sell at a loss. Most manufacturers have the attitude of being the helpful, supporting supplier to the retailer, and this attitude should go both ways, even from the vantage point of the QD merchandiser.

Just think of all the inherent elements involved in a business relationship—financial stability, trust, character, reputation, ethics, volume, volume potential, mutual respect, etc. I know this seems kind of revolutionary, but it is just common sense. What does the evidence tell us? How do we react to this? Is it a good system? Is a secret system a good system? I think we would all agree that we have some problems that require solutions. To tell or not to tell—should we keep secrets? Are we mature enough to handle the truth? True closeness comes from sharing—closeness does not come from keeping secrets. We all need closeness in all areas of our lives, even in business. Are we mature enough as a country to be open in our relationships in business?

I think about my dad as an interesting example. Of all the people whom I have met in this world, I would have to place him as the best example of a fine, Christian gentleman in every way but one. He was not the head of his family; my mother ruled the house. I think that she actually wanted him to stand up to her, but he never would.

I believe that he was a perfect model of how people can become very successful in their business life possibly while not being successful in their family life. All of his business life he worked for Rogers Department Store—over 60 years, long after retirement age. Every year that he worked he led everyone else in sales. Everyone loved Houston.

Everyone wanted Houston to wait on them. I still visualize him waiting on two, three, four or five customers at the same time and making everyone happy. Everyone loved him because he loved everyone, and he was good at what he did. Almost all of the time people will respond in kind. If you are nice to them, they are almost compelled to be nice to you.

I think that he found the love with his customers that was not reciprocated in his marriage. Being in business is very akin to going into marriage. It is a beautiful relationship when husband and wife can be close enough to share everything with each other. That wonderful warmth and closeness creates an inseparable bond, but this type of closeness must be a two-way street. If either mate has confidential areas, then that closeness is lost. Paralleling marriage, I feel strongly that we should not have secrets in business any more than we should have secrets in marriage. Possibly there are times when it must be best to compromise the truth if the other person is not emotionally mature enough to face reality with logic and reason. Can we as a society create a warm and loving, understanding and caring relationship between the manufacturer, jobber, distributor, retailer, and the customer?

YES, WE CAN!

But only with an agreed-upon set of rules to guide the relationships. We must be educated in the way that successful commerce is conducted. When the dealer's cost is public knowledge it will have the effect of keeping unscrupulous and greedy merchants from overpricing merchandise. We must be educated to understand that everyone must realize a profit in both buying and selling. Profit is the key that opens the door to prosperity. Nobody really needs excess profit, but everyone in business needs a reasonable profit. In that context, profit is not a dirty word, but loss certainly is.

Confidential dealer discounts have served to keep the American citizenry from knowing what is going on. Customers get upset when they find out that they were charged more for the same item than someone else who had bought from a merchant who had talked the supplier into "cutting a better deal."

When we do away with confidentiality we will have nothing to hide in our business relationships with one another. A whole new attitude between buyer and seller will emerge. Both buyer and seller will be helping each other to the mutual benefit of both, as well as to the benefit of society in general.

Chapter 7

THE PLAN

WHAT DO WE DO NOW? WHAT'S THE SOLUTION?

When we determine that something is not working, we need to change it. You know the old saying: "practice makes perfect;" well, that is not always the case. Many times music students just practice their mistakes. If you practice your mistakes for hours and hours, you will not get any better. You will not improve. Fifteen minutes of practicing to correct those mistakes would accomplish much more. In business we are practicing our mistakes when we continue with the QD system.

Just who is responsible for allowing QD to gain such a deleterious foothold? Manufacturers? Retailers? Jobbers? Mass merchandisers? The buying public? Government? To some degree, the answer is all of the above. As a civilized people, we must have a set of rules (or laws) to live by so that we may come together in harmony to transact daily activities and to help one another. If we are remiss in making and enforcing such a set of rules or laws, then people will be tempted to take advantage of others for their own selfish, personal gain.

I have thought long and hard about this. I have observed time and time again that, when most people perceive that a big problem exists that affects communities and even society at large, the immediate reaction is to call for some sort of government legislation. I must admit that this was my first idea. A national law and/or state laws to level the playing field by requiring manufacturers to standardize their prices for all retailers would certainly be one way to correct the problem. But would it be the best way? Maybe so; maybe not. All too often, laws have unintended consequences that turn out to be worse than the original situation.

There are other possibilities that might work just as well, and maybe even better. One approach would be to let the business world discipline itself based on an appeal to highest levels of ethics and morality and the overall good of society. Another approach is something addressed in a number of magazines and journals in recent years, and that is the charge to small business owners to focus on related aspects of their business that aren't necessarily swallowed up by the big box merchants and where they can build profit niches that are not hampered by QD.

A ONE PRICE SYSTEM

The main goal, I firmly believe, is the establishment of a one price system. Manufacturers and distributors are kidding themselves about making a profit by selling their products at huge discounts to mass merchandisers. Certainly there is some validity to the concept of being able to sell a large volume, single shipment order for less; however, an honest, realistic cost appraisal will prove that those savings are minute in comparison with the quantity discounts currently prevailing within the industry. Consider the number of manufacturers who have "gone broke" or who are in serious financial trouble because of selling too much of their product at unrealistically low prices through multilevel quantity discounts and under-the-table deals.

A bold one price approach would totally change the music industry, as well as other industries, allowing the free market to determine consumer demand rather than artificially imposed multiple discount schedules. If a manufacturer's technology and cost-cutting production and marketing methods can lower the price of the product, then lower prices would accrue to the dealers. This is how our free enterprise system is designed to work, and it continues to be the best economic system in the world.

Naturally, with these changes, there will be a transition period throughout each industry. The first manufacturers to make these pricing policy changes will be the first ones to get the dealers' orders and their loyal support. In our free country, there are no laws that dictate at what price a manufacturer must sell his product (except maybe now in the automobile industry). On the other hand, there are laws that have to do with selling to one dealer at one price and to another dealer at another price within the same trading area.

Hartley Peavey is the president of Peavey Electronics, one of manufacturing's greatest "rags to riches" stories of our time. Hartley Peavey's father was a retail music merchant, so Hartley is probably more attuned to the problems of the music industry than most. For years, Peavey Electronics had no quantity discount schedule. From the smallest dealer to the largest, Peavey dealers all paid the same price. No one got any special price consideration—not even a cash discount, factory seconds, closeouts, or under-the-table deals.

Every Peavey dealer was on equal footing with every other. Peavey's no discount integrity fostered good dealer relations. A Peavey dealership was the salvation of many merchants in recent times. In today's music marketplace, this type of dealer discount integrity was a bold approach, which contributed to the success not only of Peavey, but also to all of Peavey's dealers.[1]

Recently, however, and to the chagrin of many, Peavey has succumbed to the pressures of the QD mass merchandisers and is helping to destroy the small retailers. Peavey's previous dealer discount policy is a good model for manufacturers to adopt if they want to save the economy.

All we have to do now is determine how best to proceed. So in this penultimate chapter, I will present the pros and cons of (1) legislation; (2) self-policing by the business community; and (3) initiatives a small businessman can take to remain viable. And, of course, I would be remiss if I didn't include my own recommendations, which I will present briefly in a final chapter.

LEGISLATION

What I have found out in my research is that my idea on legislation is not that new and certainly not novel. What I would be advocating is defined in the economics field as a fair trade law, which is "any law allowing manufacturers of branded or trademarked goods (or in some instances distributors of such products) to fix the actual or minimum resale prices of these products by resellers."[2]

Early in the 20th century, there were attempts to establish such laws, all of which were found to be in violation of the Sherman Anti-Trust Act of 1890.[3] Nonetheless, circa 1911 future US Supreme Court justice Louis Brandeis assisted in the formation of the American Fair Trade League (AFTL) to bring about improvements in trade policies and laws that better protected all levels of commerce from unfair competition. According to Brandeis, ". . . the price-cutting of large department stores, mail-order catalogues, and chain stores undermined the economic, and thereby the political authority of the independent merchant"[4] The AFTL quickly became a major lobbying group, with a large membership of manufacturers and resellers across the nation.

As noted earlier, there already exist many laws and regulations that affect small business, indeed, all business. Dozens of environmental regulations fall into this category. Various labor, advertising, and online business laws can also bear on the mom-and-pop stores and how they conduct business. However, the only laws that appear to address the issue of QD are the anti-trust laws. There are several, beginning with the Sherman Act of 1890, which actually had very little to do with trusts. Its purpose was to oppose monopolistic practices that could potentially harm competition or restrain trade.[5]

Then in 1914 the Clayton Antitrust Act was passed mainly to regulate business activities that prevented competition. It contained enforcement and remedial mechanisms that were not included in the Sherman Act.[6] Also in 1914 the Federal Trade Commission Act was passed in an effort to put some teeth into the regulation of business, to kill monopolies at their source, and to prohibit retail price-fixing (unfair competition) in interstate commerce. And of course, it established the Federal Trade Commission that we still live with today.[7] These three laws are considered to be the core federal antitrust legislation, with the objective of protecting competition.

Next came the Robinson-Patman Act of 1936 that prohibited anti-competitive practices by producers, especially price discrimination. This law is the Magna Charta of small business, the first major effort to create a level playing field. Sears had purchased a high volume of tires from Goodyear at a steep discount. A price war ensued that ruined a large number of tire dealers. Robinson-Patman limited discounts given to mass merchants that purchased huge quantities from manufacturers, with the intent of preserving the market share of independent retailers.[8]

The Miller-Tydings Act was passed in 1937 to permit states to legalize resale price maintenance, or "fair trade," and to impose prices on retail merchants that had not agreed to abide by fair trade provisions.[9] Incidentally, after the Great Depression, almost all of the states passed fair trade laws.[10] Miller-Tydings was repealed in 1975, thus ending our 40-year experiment with price-fixing.[11]

Then came the Hart-Scott-Rodino (HSR) Antitrust Improvements Act of 1976, which served to amend the Clayton Act in the area of mergers and acquisitions.[12] This act does not appear to have had much of a bearing on the current problem of QD. The previous antitrust acts, however, have a direct bearing because they "...make it illegal to conspire to restrain trade or commerce in any marketplace, regardless of size."[13] As a humble layman, it seems to me that this is exactly what the QD merchandisers are doing, restricting competition to the point where the Clayton Act and/or Robinson Patman Act could well be applied at least as a partial correction, if the current FTC were so inclined. So do we really need another law? Or should we be content with the ones we have and apply them?

There are some drawbacks to legislation. I have already noted the fact that all too often laws have unintended consequences and actually make matters worse by creating more problems than they solve. A current example of this is the Affordable Care Act, which has caused so many problems that a majority of Americans want the law repealed.[14] Look it up. One renowned economist, Thomas Sowell, says that politicians today know so little about business that any law they produced would be a wrecking ball: "I would love to have a constitutional amendment that says politicians are not allowed to intervene in the economy under any circumstances."[15]

Then, there's the matter of enforcing laws. In recent years, our government has failed to enforce a number of very important laws, such as our immigration and border security requirements and the care of our servicemen and women through the Veterans Administration system. It seems as though the enforcement of laws depends more on political expediency than real justice. For example, the Obama Administration has actually encouraged and facilitated the breaking of our immigration laws, e.g., urging large numbers of illegals to cross the borders unimpeded and transporting them all over the country, condoning sanctuary cities, failing to prosecute businesses that employ illegals, doing nothing about foreigners overstaying their visas, and granting amnesty to many illegals in direct violation of the Constitution.

We saw our federal government in 2009, under the ATF's Project Gunrunner (the Fast and Furious phase), approve the illegal sales of some 2000 firearms to drug cartels in Mexico, which resulted in the death of at least two Border Patrol agents.[16] Then, we have Planned Parenthood attempting to sell the body parts of aborted fetuses in defiance of federal law. At this point, I'm not at all confident that we're a nation of laws anymore, and that's probably worse than what QD is doing to us.

But the fact remains that there are perfectly good laws to deal with this issue already on the books at both the federal and state levels. It is up to us to use them as a viable course of action to counter the QD system, even though we face the vicissitudes of the courts. As we have seen in the last 100 years, the mood swings back and forth. Perhaps it is time to restore the American Fair Trade League.

Many people feel that the least amount of government that we have the better, and I know exactly where they are coming from. However, who would want to live in a chaotic society without moral laws and values? Only by laws can we have our freedoms. The main function of government is to protect us. And only through moral and equitable laws can that protection be accomplished. Of course, I feel that the laws should be few, but just and fair. The big thing is to grasp the "spirit of the law" in the way we conduct ourselves, both in our business and our personal lives.

SELF-POLICING BY THE BUSINESS COMMUNITY

Retailers are very appreciative to manufacturers and distributors for all of the many constructive things they have done in the past. We are appreciative of the manufacturers who have run major publication advertisements designed to solicit public support for service-oriented local music retailers. This is wonderful! We only ask that manufacturers do the same thing that they are asking others to do by supporting their "root-hair" retailers with a one price discount structure.

Without the one price structure, more and more dealers are destined to fail, especially in the current recession. It's a sad and emotional experience to see any individual retailer fail. As of this date, I have personally bought out the stocks of 35 other music stores that have gone out of business. I have seen firsthand the trials and tribulations of those retailers.

When we step back and take an overview of our nation's business situation today, we can see that the woes of the music merchant are not unique. Manufacturers' and distributors' multi-level discount policies in all types of other industries have turned the mass merchandising discounters into the major vendors of our time. The result is a depressed economy and massive unemployment. Maybe, just maybe, if we could clean up our act in the music industry, we could become the role model for restoring our nation's prosperity.

Manufacturers, distributors and retailers must become a team. You manufacturers got us into this mess, and you can get us out of it—you can restore the marketplace. You can take the initiative. We need your innovative response. Should the hometown service-oriented music retailer die, the manufacturer may not be the one with the smoking gun; however, he has certainly supplied the ammunition with his multi-level discounts.

WHAT SHOULD THE MANUFACTURER AND DISTRUBUTOR DO?

1. Institute a one price discount policy for all retailers. No off-season deals. No "under-the-table" deals. No cash discounts in excess of a realistic 1% or 2%. No closeout specials. No free merchandise with large sized orders. No rebates. No free freight. In other words, close up all the loopholes that would set up any type of price differential between large volume discount houses, mail order and/or Internet outlets, and local retailers.

2. Establish the same type of one price discount policy for all of the jobbers.

3. Adopt the policy of selling only to bonafide retail outlets where the specialized product(s) may be properly presented, demonstrated and serviced by qualified personnel.

4. Never announce price changes in advance of the actual price change so that certain retailers might be able to load up at lower prices.

5. Price products in order to earn a fair and reasonable profit. This does NOT imply that there should be any attempt to fix or set retail prices. A manufacturer should determine the cost of production and distribution of the product and then

add a reasonable profit margin in establishing the suggested retail selling price. Such a one price system will restore profits to many marginal manufacturers and distributors.

6. Do not advertise in the same media whose practice it is to accept the advertisements of the mass merchandising discounters.

7. Give greater attention to redesigning and improving products as well as developing new products of high quality and utility. In the music industry, there is little or no obsolescence of the really good band and orchestral instruments. Most instruments and electronics are being produced off-shore, and they often don't compare favorably with, for example, the old vintage instruments that are now commanding premium prices.

8. Get the executives out of their "ivory towers" and back in touch with the real world. Re-discover who the customers are and where the competition is coming from. Educate the dealers on the latest in product knowledge and sales techniques. Apply technology to compete successfully with foreign-made goods.

WHAT SHOULD THE RETAILER DO?

1. Encourage manufacturers and suppliers to discontinue quantity discounts so that all vendors pay the same wholesale price for the same item.

2. Cut store overhead so that retailers can be competitive with the mass merchandisers. Decide to be either a large or a small operation, as it is almost impossible to make a profit in between.

3. Advertise your competitiveness and really "sell" your local services. In the music business, you might provide teaching facilities, repair service, instrument care workshops. Expanding your repair department and reputation as a service-

oriented dealer may be the only way to have a profitable operation if manufacturers continue their multi-level discount policies.

4. Refuse to sell and support music magazines that advertise the mass merchandising discounters.

5. Concentrate purchases from those suppliers who support the service oriented retailers with a one price discount structure.

6. Promote, promote, promote to the extent your budget will allow. Sell the benefits, special qualities, and unique features and value of your products and services.

7. Where you profitably can do so, buy the used equipment for sale by individuals in your trading area. This will help put the profit on the sale of refurbished equipment in the dealer's pocket and help prevent a buyer's market from developing. Your new profit niche may be in the sales and rentals of used and refurbished instruments.

8. Create a friendly relationship with other retailers. Realize that they are not the real competitors. The competitors to the music industry are the automobile dealers, the motorcycle dealers, computer and video games, the clothing industry, drugs and all the other businesses vying for the customer's time and money.

9. Control your inventory and keep your purchases in correct relationship with your realistic market potential. There are now some excellent computer programs available to make this task easier, quicker, and more accurate. No longer can most retailers afford to be dumped on by submitting to multi-level master orders which lead to overstocked dealers who must seek extended terms at high interest rates, not to mention the deterioration of the merchandise as it ages on the stock room shelves. Retailers should be able to realize a fair return on their investment.

THE GOVERNMENT'S ROLE

Federal, state, and local governments must support brick and mortar merchants, not tax them to death. That's really all that needs to be said on this point, but I will add a little more anyway.

We must think long range at all times. There is something inherently wrong when I can ship out of state and not charge any sales tax just as long as I do not have a storefront or a representative in that state. In a manner of speaking, I am rewarded for not giving service. If there is going to be a tax, it needs to be a uniform tax. Here in Montgomery, Alabama, they have increased the sales tax rate to 10%, which is particularly devastating on high ticket item sales.

How about Internet retailers who don't have to pay any sales tax, except in just a few states? One answer might be to place a 15% tax on Internet retail sales in an effort to encourage customers toward service oriented retail establishments physically in the community. As it is now, it is not fair to retail commerce to have to compete with almost no overhead Internet retailers who don't pay sales tax and who are not geographically located to give service to the local customer.

So our tax structure definitely needs attention, and that is clearly up to government.

HOW WOULD THIS APPROACH WORK?

On December 31st of each year, the manufacturer will release his price and must maintain that price for one year. No collusion between manufacturers will be allowed. Neither website releases of ultimate retailer prices nor mail-outs on such pricing will be allowed until 12-31. Any defective or "second quality" products must be available to all retailers—no one retailer or group of retailers can have an unequal share of such merchandise.

There will be no **confidential** price to any retailer; it must be a publicized price for all to see. The manufacturer not only sets the retail purchase price, but he also sets a suggested retail price, which he cannot reduce when selling directly to consumers or to Internet sites. Retailers, however, would be permitted to sell at less than the suggested price. The manufacturer has to realize that his pricing structure makes way for the retailer to make a reasonable profit above his cost on the item.

There would be no need for confidentiality any longer since QD mass merchants and all retailers pay the same price. Today, people think that the merchandise costs less to a dealer than it actually does. The public must be educated to realize that a profit must be made but not an excessive profit. Only when a profit is being made can the employer have the resources to pay employees a reasonable wage and sustain his business. Profit is the motivator in a capitalistic economy.

There will be no cash discounts or "gifts." If a manufacturer or distributor is not confident of the ability or trust in the dealer to pay for the merchandise or service, then the supplier may ask for payment before or upon delivery of the product. But, no cash discounts—the purpose of this is to truly level the playing field. This will help the manufacturer to be profitable by not having to decrease his profit through cash discounts or QDs. This will strengthen the spirit of the system.

Similarly, there will be no items "kicked in" by modifying the product for selected dealers. A manufacturer could do this on his own (without legislation) should he have the wisdom and motivation to do so. All you have to do is say "we do not discriminate; every dealer pays exactly the same." The only difference is that the farther the dealer is from the manufacturer or distributor the more the freight costs. This is largely a function of geography and would be an acceptable variable as long as the base price remains constant for all retailers. This assumes that the freight charges are calculated carefully and honestly. Of course, you could set a policy of no freight charges to anyone, just so you have that policy for all dealers. But if a manufacturer is producing very heavy equipment or a product where shipping cost is a huge factor, it would probably not be feasible to have a no-freight policy. This would have the side effect of encouraging the dealer to buy from a closer supplier.

The key is there are to be no exceptions. The pricing structure must be the same for all. Should you find that your policy for this one year is not working out, you can change the price of products and/or services rendered to the dealers on December 31st for the next year.

TRANSITION PERIOD

When the revised system is implemented, the full impact will not be felt immediately because a quantity of products previously purchased will still be on the shelves. The full effects of the system would not be felt until the old product is sold and the new system products begin to take over the market. This may not take all that long, however, as "just in time" merchandising has left many suppliers with rather minimal inventories actually in stock. However, many types of merchants do not have that fast a turnover.

If a manufacturer chooses to extend credit to the retailer, payment from the retailer should be made within 30 days with a maximum of 60 days at most. I realize that this book is full of radical ideas, but when you think them through you will see that this course correction must take place to restore some sanity and fairness. If the manufacturer is not paid within 60 days then late charges may be levied on the dealer.

What we need to develop is a nation of experts— specialists in their field of merchandising. One reason that the public will seek you out to buy from you is because you know more about the manufacturing, sales, service, repair, and maintenance than anyone else. But, in spite of all that, your price needs to be competitive. When you become that type of person, you have a great feeling of self-satisfaction and personal worth. You become driven for even greater growth, service and satisfaction in both your business and your personal life.

After the initial period where things will settle out and merchandise previously purchased under QD is sold, then everyone will be paying the same wholesale price for the merchandise. Accordingly, small dealer retail prices can come down to more competitive levels. Additionally, because of the resourcefulness of small business entrepreneurship, it is likely that those prices could come down even more, as many existing businesses already own their building and have already paid for their fixtures, furniture, and equipment. In other words, they quite possibly might have less overhead to contend with.

Those retailers may even be able to be profitable at prices less than what the mass merchandisers are selling the product for at that time. However, should the price go up a bit more than this, the buying public must be educated to realize that they would be giving employment to thousands of Americans who were not working previously. That means that many of those workers have come off the government's rolls of the unemployed. Every news source I'm aware of has been reporting that some 94M capable Americans are not working today.

The super rich must realize that their wealth has come from QD. Their monopolistic endeavors have invaded every industry. If they love our country enough and can see the "big picture," they will realize that they took somewhat unfair advantage of small business in making that wealth by the faulty system of quantity discounts. They can now show outgoing concern for and love of their fellow man by altruistically giving the masses an opportunity to be as successful as they are. The starting point is the manufacturer, who must be willing to hold the line.

But can it be done? Can we rely on the fundamental goodness of our fellow man to pull it off? Some do not believe so. Consider what happened in the late 1990s when it was announced that the Clinton Administration would have a surplus of some $360B, and many clamored for a rebate to the taxpayers. (In fact, there was no surplus after all, as some of the Social Security Trust Fund had been moved to the General Fund to give the appearance of a surplus;

instead there was a deficit of $281B, and the national debt rose to $5.8T.[17]) Clinton stated "that he wouldn't consider giving it back to the taxpayers because they couldn't be trusted to spend it right."[18] Noted author Ann Coulter says, "American businesses are like sharks: All appetite, no brain. They're willing to screw over everyone in their line of sight to make one more dollar in profit."[19]

As for me, I have more faith in my fellow man and fellow businessman than this.

SMALL BUSINESS INITIATIVES

Today's trade journals typically carry articles on how to outsmart the QD merchandisers by developing profit niches that the big-box stores can't readily duplicate and taking advantage of the unique qualities that are characteristic of small business. "There are still opportunities for a small town, single-store music dealer. You probably won't get extremely wealthy; in fact, you probably won't even get moderately rich. However, if you play your cards right, you will make a well-above-average income doing something that is fun, and you'll get a tremendous amount of satisfaction in the process."[20]

What I am going to cover here primarily applies to the music industry, but there is general relevance to other industries as well. Here is the prevailing wisdom in the music industry:

1. Use community involvement to counter the big-box impact. This really is your ace in the hole, because the mass merchants aren't going to do this.

    a. Make presentations to school assemblies, emphasizing the importance of music and its benefits.
    b. Provide youth workshops, demonstrating the various instruments and what they sound like.
    c. Hold music fairs and invite accomplished groups to perform.
    d. Sponsor competitions in the schools and in the community. Sponsor a community band.
    e. Participate in local civic clubs and promote music education. Appeal to older musicians to be active again. Always be proactive.
    f. Provide music folders with your store logo prominently displayed.
    g. Attend in-service training sessions at schools and assist at band/orchestra camps.
    h. Visit schools regularly. Make sure your roadmen are highly qualified.

2. Take advantage of the technology age and introduce computer-based music platforms in your inventory.
3. Provide lessons and group programs for young children. Offer desirable, nicely appointed, private teaching quarters and waiting rooms.
4. Use technology to stay in touch with customers. Send out emails or use Facebook to announce promotions and coming events. Maintain an attractive and user friendly website.
5. Increase your supply of accessories. The big box stores are not going to carry reeds, mouthpieces, guitar strings, valve oil, resin for violin bows, drumsticks, etc.
6. Emphasize product differentiation in your promotions. Certain brands are always going to be better buys than

the cheap instruments sold at Walmart, price notwithstanding.

7. Fully develop your repair shop and take advantage of this unique resource; big-box stores are not going to offer this.

8. Track and manage carefully your inventory. Check computer summaries at least weekly to know what you have on hand and what you need to order. In past years, I never worried about excess inventory, because it was like "money in the bank." If we did not sell it this year, no big deal; it would appreciate in value because of inflation and be worth still more the next year. Today there is no way I can look at inventory the same as in the past.

9. Maintain your store like you would your home—clean and pleasant. Make it look inviting.

10. Focus primarily on your customers.[21]

11. Support local efforts to redevelop small towns and communities. Allow me to elaborate on this one. In a number of locales, there has begun such a move to reverse the migration to large cities, to direct business away from the mass merchandisers, and to restore the availability of quality American goods as an alternative to cheap goods manufactured in China. These communities are issuing their own currency, like Detroit Cheer, Bay Bucks, Berkshares, and Ithaca Hours. People can buy one dollar of the local currencies for 90 or 95 cents and shop in all the stores that have agreed to accept them.[22] "As of the beginning of 2009, there were more than seventy-five local currency systems being issued across America."[23] The intent is to assure that the money spent and earned in the local community stays there. This movement "suggests a growing awareness among Americans of the need to

support U.S. businesses and U.S.-made goods in order to preserve the U.S. middle class."[24]

So perhaps the ideas presented in this chapter, and in this last section particularly, are not that farfetched. Maybe we have more control over the matter than we might think. "By sticking to what you do best and by stepping back and strategically identifying markets, products, and services ignored by big-box retailers, you can carve out a successful niche to serve in your community."[25]

This is my advice as well. I could not state it any more clearly.

Chapter 8

FINAL THOUGHTS

I don't know if it's all that wise for an 87-year-old man to be referring to "final thoughts," but I'll have to take that risk. Indulge me for a moment as I describe a scenario that has long haunted me. Too many small businesses have fallen victim to the unfair practices of larger companies. We are going to have to take our country back from the plague of QD. Unless we put restraints in place to kill QD, we must consider where the QD system will take us. Because of the very nature of QD, it will eventually result in self-destruction.

Here's how: The rich will get richer as their QD-based enterprises get bigger and bigger, taking over all of the commercial sectors one by one. These mass merchandisers have the resources to be able to embrace the ultimate in technology—technology that takes the place of people (loss of jobs), not to mention their proclivity for outsourcing any function of their business that might be done cheaper in another nation all the way on the other side of the world. These ultimate efficiencies will improve their profits but at the expense of jobs for American workers. When it ends up that a small handful of mass QD merchants kills the rest of the small business world, there will be hardly any jobs left to be had. Without the income from jobs, there will be no money to buy products even in the QD mass merchants' stores. At that point we will have total economic collapse: QD self-destruction. This is perhaps an over simplification but an excursion that deserves attention.

Theoretically, if we project it out to the end, it might become possible that one person could end up owning the nation's sales economy—the person who has enough money to buy more wholesale merchandise than everyone else so that he could sell it cheaper than anyone else, and the buying public would beat a path to his door to get that lowest price.

Unless something changes, our nation is headed for the biggest economic collapse that the world has ever known.

Think about it: As of the writing of this book we have close to $20 trillion of national debt. Total debt—which includes household and business debt plus debt at all levels of government—stands at $66.6T.[1] Our kids are inheriting a tremendous debt load. Our nation is owned by foreign countries. If they called in the loans, there is no way we can pay them back. It would not be to their advantage to shut us down because we still have purchasing power. The dollar has eroded tremendously, and as we print money without anything to back it, its value will erode that much more. The thing that is keeping us alive is the fact that the interest rate is being kept artificially low so that the money that comes in the month before pays the loan interest along with all the other myriad government checks.

The public needs to be educated to look at a Walmart store and realize that this is part of the system that could destroy our economy. The basic foundation of the mass merchandiser is built on faulty footings—QD in other words. How rich you are determines what price you pay for your merchandise. As you get still richer, you are able to expand into taking over other industries, and in theory if you have enough money you could take over everything and own the whole retail industry. I could name several individuals or cabals in the world that are actively striving to do this; I'll let you fill in the blanks. We must change the rules so that this does not come to pass.

I recognize that many of you will regard the foregoing as mere hyperbole, and I may be wrong—I truly hope so. But it is possible that I may be right. One of the principles I have always tried to apply in my life is to see things through to the end, project events to their logical conclusion. I am probably no better at predicting the future than anyone else, but again, I just might be right.

QD causes loss of retail jobs—therefore increasing unemployment rates. While the Bureau of Labor Statistics claims the current rate is only 5.6%, presidential candidates are revealing that the actual rate is much higher. One says it is really 10.5%[2] and another says it's between 18% and 20%[3]. I believe that it's probably much more than 20%. Whichever figure you want to go with, too many people are out of work.

With further regard to QD, bigger is not necessarily better. In fact, as your business grows larger, it is a great challenge to maintain the quality, level of service, and expertise that built the business in the first place. As business gets bigger, it is very difficult to get people motivated and trained to be able to have the expertise and fervor of the founder—particularly so when a business is forced to keep wages low to help keep prices low. Under these circumstances, it is very, very hard to motivate these employees to the higher standards that initially built the business.

Our companies are making a profit today by selling cheap-priced merchandise from other countries made by cheap foreign labor. But all of that profit is being made at the expense of the American worker who has lost his job or has taken a lesser paying job to be able to subsist and feed his family. I hear constantly on TV and the radio that there are some 94M capable Americans not working

.
We cannot afford to continue to let this happen to the American worker. This is one of the main reasons we have government, so that laws may be passed and enforced to

protect the citizens of our country. It's hard to be all things to all people. Super QD stores can't do the job of serving like a specialty business, where they are knowledgeable in their area of expertise. When employees practice poor business techniques they don't get better—like a musician practicing his mistakes.

We must rebuild business opportunities for small business by outlawing quantity discounts and leveling the playing field.[4] Anything done for one retailer has to be done for all others. We must consider implementing higher duties on imports from foreign countries and possibly doing away with the current sales tax system. If we are going to continue our sales tax system, then it needs to be a level tax for everyone and everything, including the Internet.

If the solutions recommended in this book had been implemented years ago, many great stores and the great services they rendered might still be in existence. It is imperative that we stop the death and destruction of our small business retail community.

Consider the distress of service-oriented businesses, which are devastated and destroyed because the super rich, quantity discount dealers, using their wealth, are able to beat the manufacturers down in price so that no one can compete with them. It is absolutely vital that our government protects its citizenry, manufacturers, and small retailers from the business tyranny of the super rich. Adequate laws are already in place. It's equally important that the business community take steps to discipline itself for the good of the country. And finally, small dealers have to rework their business plans to focus on those relevant and feasible niches not being served by the big box stores.

Just think about those brave and noble souls who go into business, work long and hard to make the business successful, and serve the public well, only to have their enterprises gutted through no fault of their own. Thousands and thousands of new and long-established retailers are being forced daily into bankruptcy—forced to sell or liquidate their stores for pennies on the dollar. Unless stemmed quickly, this destruction of small business will have a lasting deleterious impact not only on the economy, but on families, entire communities, and the very fabric of American society.

Every businessman, whether he knows it or not, has a set of principles to guide his planning and daily decisions and actions. There are four things I have always tried to live my life by:

1. **Think things through to the end**. In management and military circles, this is called strategic thinking. I try to envision the outcome of everything I do. In my business, I go over and above expectations. This is what builds customer loyalty in any endeavor; this is what made my business successful. What are the results? Capitol Music in, of all places, "little old Montgomery, Alabama," was voted one of the top 50 music stores in America (out of the 8,400-plus music dealers in America).[5] This principle has served me well.

2. **Instantly forgive**. There is not a person alive who has not been hurt or harmed by another individual or group. This has happened to me many, many times, but by instantly forgiving I have been able to go forward without cumbersome grudges to maintain my strategic perspective: keeping the main thing the main thing. The one thing that has grown my business is giving expertise and exceptional service to others. Most people in this old world will normally respond in kind. If you are nice to them, most of the time they will be nice to you. Customer satisfaction is the best type of advertisement,

and there is no way that you can buy it; you have to earn it by working for it and doing the best you can do in everything that you do.

3. **See things in perspective**. This is intimately related to the previous two principles, but the difference is that this one entails considering every side, every facet, of any issue that arises. These considerations affect the determination of outcomes in strategic planning, as well as the manner in which you forgive. Sometimes, you even have to forgive yourself. Personally, it gives me a special feeling of satisfaction knowing that I may be one of the best musical instrument repairmen in the world. I always try to do the very best work that can be done. I try to achieve the same high level of craftsmanship, whether this is for a top professional musician or a beginning student in school.

We all can develop skills in our work. I can make a saxophone "sing," but it takes a long time to learn. There's not enough lifetime to learn everything about everything. We are forced to specialize—to become an expert so that we can barter our skills in one area with another person who has skills in another area. If you have specialized skills and try to be the best there is, you should never have any trouble locating a job; you will always be in demand as long as the economy survives.

4. **Don't depend on others for happiness**. Unless one lives as a hermit, there are people constantly coming in and out of our lives. Every one of them has different attitudes, skills, and opinions, and they may not coincide with yours. Those people may make you happy, or they may aggravate you, sometimes intensely. What I try to remember is that I am the only one who can decide if I'm happy or not. Nobody else can make this decision for me. I have found that it's always easier and certainly more rewarding to be happy and optimistic than it is to be sad. That's why I try to instantly forgive. My work is mainly what makes me happy.

I am writing this page late at night, at 1:30 a.m. (past midnight), having just finished over 4 hours of work on a brand new, top of the line, professional, French-made clarinet. This was a work of love to take this instrument to a mechanical and musical level much higher than the way it came from the factory. Several of the keys were refitted, pads seated to perfection, and spring tension readjusted to the feel that the player preferred. All of this type of work requires special skills and a tremendous amount of patience. I have taken the instrument to a still higher level of perfection. The joints were built up to eliminate any hint of wobble. All of this type of work has built an almost international reputation for my service. This is the type of craftsmanship that is becoming more and more scarce. Are you going to get this type of special skill and service from the mass merchandise QD company? I don't think so!

THE SHOE BRUSH

This is a short story that I hope serves as an analogy to the relatively brief, yet crucially important, role we have in the history of a noble country and economy that we trust will live on long after we're gone and for generations to come. I bought a shoe brush some 65 years ago from Rogers Department Store in Florence, Alabama. It was a really good shoe brush, for back then quality products were made to last. Rogers Department Store where I bought the brush is no longer in business, but the brush lives on. Probably the workman who made the brush is dead, but the brush lives on. When I bought the brush, all shoes were made of leather, and I loved the "spit shine" the brush produced. The brush is bound to have shined shoes over 20,000 times. It has shined thousands of clarinet bodies. It's a bit worn but still in perfectly useable condition. The amount paid for the brush was small, possibly the best return on investment that I have ever made. Every indication is that the brush will outlive me and will serve for generations to come if passed down in the family. This is the kind of enduring quality that "made in America" should signify.

The price of any product or service, however, can override the best of service or quality. That's why we must level the business playing field so that the purchase price will not vary that much from dealer to dealer. Anyone would rather buy from the dealer giving the best service and selection if there is not too much difference in the purchase price. When we neutralize QD, we level the business playing field.

In an open, competitive business environment the amount of profit that you can make is what the customer is willing to pay. Keep this in mind–if all the retailers are paying the same price for the merchandise, then the competitive market will determine what profit can be made. If you attempt to charge too much, then the customers are not going to buy from you unless you give some type of extra service that makes buying from you worth the extra price.

The key to all of this is to level the playing field so that all the retailers are paying the same price for the goods that they will be selling. On the retail level this will encourage better service, extra value, and competitive pricing from the retailer. The retailer will be rewarded with more sales for good service, quality, and knowledgeable sales people. With all retailers, regardless of size, paying the same price for the merchandise, this will automatically keep the super rich from being able to dominate the market.

This will give an equal opportunity for the young, new entrepreneurs to be successful in the market place. This means that thousands of new businesses will be profitable and existing business can again be profitable. The trickle up effect will increase employment everywhere. Manufacturers, jobbers, and distributors will be profitable and our national economy will take off like a rocket into space. No longer will the manufacturers be beaten down by the rich QD merchants–the manufacturer can again become profitable without gouging the small guys. Our American manufacturers can't afford to take what they have been forced to take from the super rich QD merchants. They must be liberated.

We Americans have great ambition and tremendous drive. Give us half a chance and we will succeed and survive. Look at the history of our country; we are survivors. We must restore a business environment that will perpetuate the American dream. We have to give our young people, those coming after us, the opportunity to succeed and build an even greater legacy and achieve their American dream.

MY CHALLENGE TO YOU

Under the Constitution, we have the right and freedom to choose the type of community that we would want to live in and pursue our dreams as we see fit. Read this book with an open mind in spite of preconceived thoughts and ideas. This book is designed to outline the progressively small steps by which massive economic change can be effected. Change your mind if you see it is the right thing to do, and act responsibly for the future of our country.

But it is going to take courage and endurance to achieve these changes. We only have a small window of time to get this accomplished. It's now only a matter of time. Much publicity has been given to the financial demise of the middle class American. We need to unite our United States. This book is honest and, of necessity, it is blunt.

There is too big a gap between the rich and the poor in America, a growing divide, in large measure due to QD. At times, we seem to be hell-bent on the destruction of our economy. I hope that this book will inspire leaders in every segment of society to bring us out of this demise. QD only works to the advantage of big business—only to the advantage of the very rich, to make them richer.

We have to believe in the future generation. We have got to do what is necessary today so that they will have the opportunity tomorrow. It is not too late to change. We must change in order to avoid the destruction of what is left of the American economy. Small business is the backbone of the American economy and must have some protection and fair treatment. Our country is too great and has too much potential to let this happen to us.

In December, 1955, just months after my wife and I had opened our new music store in downtown Montgomery, Alabama, there was an incident out front at the bus stop. Rosa Parks refused to give up her seat and move to the back of the bus. That small act changed the entire country for the better. We all know what happened. Now we have a situation where small business has been relegated to the "back of the bus." What I am doing is speaking up for the average American brick and mortar merchant. Someone has to stand up for what is right. Someone has to be our Rosa Parks. Someone has to draw attention to the economic segregation resulting from quantity discounts. I would like to leave the world a better place. My mission is to present ideas that can bring about effective change.

We need a conciliatory relationship between supplier and retailer—not the adversarial QD relationship. This is an issue of reform. I have waited this long to present this book because I wanted to wait until the QD system had run its course—waiting for the time that any thinking and observant person could readily see where we are headed. This book is timely. It should be heeded now and not be deferred until a complete economic collapse.

One of the purposes of this book has been to educate and inform the public about what is going on in the business world, how our "system" now works. An informed public can have the power to demand reform and the remedial procedures to bring a halt. Let's flush all the old rules of manufacturer, jobber, distributor, and retailer confidential pricing down the toilet. Let's start all over again and do it in an open, honest and fair way. Let's do it the real American way. Let's make business honest and straightforward.

The time has come for the small business community and the public at large to take a stand before the economic collapse of our nation occurs. We can have our place in history or we can continue to blindly go down the path of destruction with quantity discounts. Either we control things or those things will control us. The implementation of the solutions presented in this book could very likely be the salvation of our economy. Somehow, I strongly feel that my life has given me the background, the experience and the "calling," if you will, to get this message out. Possibly I was destined to do this book, and I am greatly honored and humbled to have had the opportunity to present these thoughts and ideas. I have attempted to share with you the inner workings, the business "secrets," the joys and the sadness, the opportunities, the heart and soul of the American worker and small business entrepreneur.

Tonight, I am writing this in a restaurant just after having attended a school band concert in a smaller town just north of Montgomery. Going to concerts is part of my job, and I would be very conspicuous by my absence if I were not there. The band director in this school is very good but very firm— the kind of director whom, years later, the former students come back to, hug his neck, and express how much they appreciate all that he did to put them on the right track in life.

This was a spring concert and the last concert the seniors would be playing in high school. It was somewhat of a tradition that the students would "surprise" the band director with a gift; however, the band president apologized to the director explaining that the gift that they had ordered for him had not come in. She went on to say how much band had meant to her. Just before putting the microphone down she turned around to the band and asked if anyone else would like to say something. Spontaneously, unrehearsed, several of the graduating seniors came forward to take the microphone. You could tell that the kids were a bit shy talking over the PA system, but it did not dampen their sincere, heartfelt remarks.

Keep in mind that some of these students came from broken homes, and it is possible that the band director is the nearest thing to a noble, "God-fearing" type of father that they will ever have. These kids exemplify the "all American" good kids. Some broke down, and tears came to their eyes as they poured out their heartfelt appreciation of their relationship with the director, their teachers, the administration and their fellow students. I don't think that there were many dry eyes in the audience by the time the last one spoke. We can't let these old fashioned, exemplary, all-American, kids down. We have to make the changes outlined in this book so that they all will have a chance at the all-American dream. Some of these kids will go to college, some will not. College is not necessarily for everyone. Regardless, they will be going out into the world to pursue the American dream—a dream that is hardly achievable any longer because of the curse of QD. These are good kids—kids who can be successful if given a decent chance in life. We must put the solutions in place to remove the obstacles in their way to achieving success in life.

My dear friends, I hope that I have achieved what I set out to do in writing this book. It is now your call. It is going to be up to you to help get these solutions implemented. I'm just the "Paul Revere." Once we have gotten the message out, all of us will have to be the soldiers to win this war to save our businesses and help create an exciting new and successful nation.

NOTES

Chapter 1

[1]SBA Office of Advocacy. "Frequently Asked Questions About Small Business," www.sba.gov/advocacy, March 2014.

Chapter 2

[1] *Compton's Pictured Encyclopedia*, F.E. Compton & Company, Chicago IL, 1959, Vol. 1, pp. 202-205.

[2] Ibid., pp. 213, 220-221, 226.

[3] Ibid., pp. 214, 218, 220-221.

[4] Ibid., pp. 221, 230.

[5] Ibid., Vol. 7, pp. 168, 172, 174.

[6] Ronda, James P. *Lewis and Clark Among the Indians*, University of Nebraska Press, Lincoln NE, 1984, pp. xv, xviii.

[7] *Compton's*, Ibid., Vol. 12, pp. 72-74

[8]http://www.thehistoryworkshop.com/files/snagboat/10and11/ahistoryofsteamboats.pdf.

[9]http://eh.net/encyclopedia/article/nonnenmacher.industry.telegraphic.us.

[10] *Compton's*, Ibid., Vol. 7, pp. 176-177, 179.

[11] http://www.netmba.com/mgmt/scientific/

[12] *Compton's*, Ibid., p. 74.

[13] http://en.wikipedia.org/wiki/Government_Bridge.

[14]http://www.archive.org/stream/whenlincolnfough00alle/whenlincolnfough00alle_djvu.txt.

[15] *Compton's*, Ibid., p. 79.

[16] http://en.wikipedia.org/wiki/The_Music_Man.

[17]http://pages.cms.k12.nc.us/gems/justinholt/EssentialQuestionAnswers.doc.

[18] http://www.brookesnews.com/080812obamarecession.html.

[19] http://www.u-s-history.com/pages/h1661.html.

[20] *Compton's*, Ibid. p. 180.

[21]http://www.america.gov/st/business-english/2006/January/20080814215602XJyrreP0.6187664.html.

[22] http://uncpress.unc.edu/browse/page/220.

[23] http://economics.about.com/od/smallbigbusiness/a/small_business.htm.

[24] Corsi, Jerome. *America for Sale*, Threshold Editions, New York NY, 2009, p. 97.

[25] http://www.businessweek.com/smallbiz/content/nov2009/sb20091112_157141.htm.

[26] http://www.askjim.biz/answers/small-business-employment_517.php.

[27] http://www.adpemploymentreport.com/.

[28] http://online.wsj.com/article/SB122576077569495545.html.

[29] Gingrich, Newt, *To Renew America*, Harper Collins Publishers, New York NY, 1995, p. 81.

Chapter 3

(None)

Chapter 4

[1] Crews, Clyde Wayne. "The Federal Register Topped 70,000 Pages Today," November 24, 2014, Competitive Enterprise Institute, https://cei.org/blog/federal-register-topped-700000-pages-today.

[2] Santorum, Rick. "Stop Crushing Economy with Regulations," *Greenville News* (South Carolina), January 16, 2012.

[3] "Industry Ingenuity on Display," *The Music Trades*, January 2012, p. 88.

[4] Neefus, Chris. "FDA Says it Will Take Vending Machine Owners an Extra 14 Million Hours a Year to Comply with Obamacare Calorie Mandate," www.cnsnews.com, Nov. 8, 2010; and Bakst, Daren. "Obamacare's Menu Labeling Law: The Food Police Are Coming," www.heritage.org, Aug. 6, 2013.

[5] Shane, Scott. "Small Business's Problem with Government Regulation," *Small Business Trends*, January 31, 2011.

[6] Suddath, Claire. "It's Illegal for Monks to Sell Caskets in Louisiana," www.bloomberg.com, June 1, 2012.

[7] Goldwert, Lindsay. "Cash-strapped Philly: Bloggers must pay for business license," www.nydailynews.com, Aug. 23, 2010.

[8] "The high cost of going out of business," https://spellchek.wordpress.com, May 13, 2013.

[9] "Labor and Labor Unions," *Compton's Pictured Encyclopedia*, Vol. 8, F.E. Compton & Company, Chicago IL, 1959. p. 86.

[10] "Samuel Gompers," *Compton's*, Ibid., Vol. 6, p. 157.

[11] "Labor and Labor Unions," *Compton's*, Ibid., Vol. 8, pp. 87-91.

[12] Greenhouse, Stephen. "Union Membership in U.S. Fell to a 70-Year Low Last Year," *The New York Times*, Jan. 21, 2011.

[13] Savage, Michael. *Trickle Up Poverty*, HarperCollins Publishers, New York NY, 2010, pp. 99-100.

[14] Majeski, Brian T. "Thoughts on the Future of Retail," *The Music Trades*, January 2012, p. 20.

[15] "Industry Ingenuity on Display," *The Music Trades*, Jan. 2012, p. 85.

[16] Solis, Brian. "No Business is Too Big to Fail or Too Small to Succeed," http://www.briansolis.com, Feb. 28, 2013.

Chapter 5

[1] SBA Office of Advocacy. "Frequently Asked Questions About Small Business," http://www.sba.gov/advocacy, March, 2014.

[2] Cornwall, Jeff. "New Data Show the Scope of Small Business in US Economy," www.drjeffcornwall.com/2005/08, August 5, 2005.

[3] Majeski, Brian T. "Henry Ford And Steve Jobs . . . Retail Revolutionaries," *Music Trades*, August 2015, p. 24.

[4] Bean, Jonathan J. *Beyond the Broker State: Federal Policies Toward Small Business, 1936-1961*, The University of North Carolina Press, Chapel Hill NC, 1996, p. 68.

[5] Levinson, Mark. "When Creative Destruction Visited the Mom-and-Pops: The A&P grocery company may be nearing its sell-by date, but a century ago it was a fresh, revolutionary business," *The Wall Street Journal*, Oct, 12, 2013, p. A13.

[6] Bergdahl, Michael. *What I Learned From Sam Walton*, John Wiley & Sons, Inc., Hoboken NJ, 2004, p. xiii.

[7] Ibid.

[8] Ibid., p. 1.

[9] Ibid., p. 2.

[10] Griffin, Ricky W. *Management*, Houghton Mifflin Co., Boston MA, 1993, pp. 292-300.

[11] US Inflation Calculator, http://www.usinflationcalculator,com, August 18, 2015.

[12] Conn-Selmer, Inc. "2013 Band & String Confidential Price List," Elkhart IN, July 1, 2013, p.17.

[13] "Historical Inflation Rate." http://www.inflationdata.com, July 17, 2015.

[14] "United States Core Inflation Rate," http://www.tradingeconomics.com, July, 2015.

[15] "US Inflation Calculator," http://www.usinflationcalculator.com.

[16] "Prices for 1955," http://www.fiftiesweb.com.

[17] "1985 Combined Car Base Information," https://www.michigan.gov/1985combca_19779_7.pdf, p.3.

[18] "1985 Economy/Prices," 1980s Flashback Economy/Prices, http://www.1980sflashback.com/economy.asp and "Prices in the Eighties," http://www.intheeighties.com/prices.html.

[19] "Producer Price Index by Industry: Musical Instrument Manufacturing: Other Musical Instruments and Parts," https://research.stlouisfed.org.

[20] "Predict Inflation with the Producer Price Index," http://www.investopedia.com/economics/11/breaking-down-producers-price-index.asp.

[21] E.K. Blessing Co., "Suggested Retail Price List," Dec. 15, 1988.

[22] Ricks, Steve. "New Horn-Yes a Darby!" http://www.trumpetmaster.com/vb/f139/new-horn-yes-darby-56559.html, Sep. 10, 2004.

[23] Ibid.

[24] "The Darby Trumpet," www.capitolmusicusa.com, 2004.

[25] "Producer Price Index by Industry: Musical Instrument Manufacturing: Other Musical Instruments and Parts," https://research.stlouisfed.org.

[26] Wilson, Reid. "Watch the US Transition from a Manufacturing Economy to a Service Economy," *The Washing Post*, www.washingtonpost.com, Sep. 3, 2014.

[27] Funding Universe. "History of Fender Musical Instruments Company" and "Bose Corporation History," http://www.fundinguniverse.com/company-histories/.

[28] Teach, Don. "Working for the Government?," *The Music Trades*, Feb. 2006, p. 16.
[29] Ibid.
[30] Ibid.

Chapter 6

[1] Bergdahl, Michael. *What I Learned from Sam Walton*, John Wiley & Sons, Inc., Hoboken NJ, 2004, p. 15.
[2] McBroom, Allen. "The MAP That Leads to You," *The Music and Sound Retailer*, Vol. 32, No. 6, June 15, 2015, p. 1.
[3] Ibid, p. 42.
[4] Ibid.
[5] *Compton's Pictured Encyclopedia*, Vol. 7, Chicago: F.E. Compton & Company, 1959, p. 177.
[6] G. Leblanc Corporation. "Confidential Dealer Discount Schedule," Zone A, Kenosha WI, Jan. 1, 1993.
[7] Conn-Selmer, Inc. "Band and String Confidential Price List," Elkhart IN, July 1, 2012.
[8] McBroom, Allen. "The MAP That Leads to You," *The Music and Sound Retailer*, Volume 32, No. 6, June 15, 2015, p. 42.
[9] Ibid., p. 43.

Chapter 7

[1] Darby, Jim. "Mr. Manufacturer: I Challenge You to Compare," *Musical Merchandise Review*, May 1999, p. 28.
[2] "Fair-trade law," *Encyclopaedia Britannica*, http://www.britannica.com/topic/fair-trade-law, Aug. 31, 2015.
[3] Ibid.
[4] Jacobs, Meg. *Pocketbook Politics: Economic Citizenship in Twentieth Century America*, Princeton University Press, Princeton NJ, 2007, p. 34.
[5] "The Antitrust Laws," Federal Trade Commission, https://www.ftc.gop/tips-advice/competition-guidance/guide-antitrust-laws/antitrust-laws.
[6] Ibid.

[7] Northrup, Cynthia Clark, ed. *The American Economy: Essays and Primary Source Documents*, ABC-CLIO, Santa Barbara CA, 2003, p. 112.

[8] Bean, Jonathan J. *Beyond the Broker State: Federal Policies Toward Small Business, 1936-1961*,The University of North Carolina Press, Chapel Hill NC, 1996, p. 17.

[9] Hovenkamp, Herbert. *The Opening of American Law: Neoclassical Legal Thought, 1970-1970*, Oxford University Press, New York NY, 2015, p. 232.

[10] Bean, Ibid., p. 72.

[11] Hovenkamp, Ibid.

[12] "The Antitrust Laws, " Ibid.

[13] SBA. "Understanding Fair Practice," http://www.sba.gov.

[14] Levin, Mark R. *Plunder and Deceit*, Threshold Editions, New York NY, 2015, pp. 63-71.

[15] Meyers, Jim, and Martella, Ashley. "Thomas Sowell: Washington's Meddling Wrecking Economy," Newsmax Media, http://www.newsmax.com/Headline/obama-economy-cain-tax/2011/10/25/id/415707/, Oct. 25, 2011.

[16] Attkisson, Sharyl. "A Primer on the 'Fast and Furious' Scandal," CBS News, Feb. 12, 2013, www.cbsnews.com/news/a-primer-on-the-fast-and-furious-scandal/.

[17] Steiner, Craig. "The Clinton Surplus Myth," http://finance.townhall.com, Aug. 22, 2011.

[18] Congressional Record-House, March 25, 1999, p. 5672.

[19] Coulter, Ann. *¡Adios America!* Regnery Publishing, Washington DC, 2015, p. 24.

[20] Popyk, Bob. "*USA Today* and the Shop Local Movement," *The Music Trades*, Jan. 2012, p. 80.

[21] Tutt, Paige. "Anniversary: Capitol Music," *Musical Merchandise Review*, July 2015, p.80-82; Vedda, Dan. "Managing Your Inventory," *The Music and Sound Retailer*, June 2008, p. 48; Bergdahl, Michael. *What I Learned from Sam Walton*, John Wiley & Sons, Inc., Hoboken NJ, 2004, pp. 94, 95, 101, 109.

[22] Corsi, Jerome. *America for Sale*, Threshold Editions, New York NY, 2009, pp. 225-227.

[23] Ibid., p. 225.

[24] Ibid., p. 226.

[25] Bergdahl, Michael. *What I Learned From Sam Walton*, John Wiley & Sons, Inc., Hoboken NJ, 2004, p. 91.

Chapter 8

[1] Federal Reserve. www.usdebtclock.org. December 26, 2016

[2] Ross, Chuck. "Bernie Sanders Says 'Real' Unemployment Rate is Actually 10.5 Percent, Double the Official Rate," *Daily Caller*, July 6, 2015, http://www.dailycaller.com/2015/07/06/bernie-sanders. . .

[3] Jacobsen, Louis. "Donald Trump says 'real' unemployment rate is 18 to 20 percent," (AP/Richard Drew), June 16, 2015, http://www.politifact.com/truth-o-meter/statements/2015/jun/16/donald-trump…

[4] Phillips, Zach. "2006: Year of the Bankruptcy," *Music Inc.*, Jan. 2007, p. 8; and DiPasquale, Frank. "Keep the Playing Field Level," *Progressive Grocer*, July 2101, p. 16.

[5] "Honor Roll," *Music Inc.*, Dec. 2004, p. 54.

www.ingramcontent.com/pod-product-compliance
Lightning Source LLC
Chambersburg PA
CBHW022015170526
45157CB00003B/1252